BENEDICT XVI
'FELLOW WORKER FOR THE TRUTH'

BENEDICT XVI
'FELLOW WORKER FOR THE TRUTH'
an introduction to his life and thought

LAURENCE PAUL HEMMING

burns & oates

Continuum

The Tower Building
11 York Road
London SE1 7NX

4775 Linglestown Road
Harrisburg
PA 17112

Burns & Oates is an imprint of Continuum Books

www.continuumbooks.com

First published 2005

British Library Cataloguing-in-Publication Data
A catalogue record for this book is available from the
British Library.

ISBN 0–86012–409–6

Designed and typeset by Benn Linfield
Printed and bound by MPG Books, Bodmin, Cornwall

for
Fr. Kit Cunningham IC, MBE
pastor bonus

*Beloved, it is a loyal thing you do
when you render any service to the brethren. So
we ought to support such men,
that we may be fellow workers
for the truth.*

3 John 1

Contents

Preface

This book is written by someone familiar with the Pope's writings, in the hope of making some of the themes in them available to a wider audience. I make no claims to objectivity for this book – if such objectivity were in any case possible. It carries no official weight – it is written by one least in the ranks of clergy. It is written only with the hope of helping the reader form a deeper, and more accurate, opinion of Pope Benedict than that perhaps with which he or she began. I hope I introduce especially those aspects of the Pope's thought which might assume greater importance as his papacy unfolds.

I have adopted the convention of referring to the Pope by the name Benedict at all points in his life. The alternatives seemed too cumbersome and confusing. It is Aristotle who teaches us that with things that belong to the physical, temporal order we only understand them fully when they have come to their fulfilment. This is why God knows us better than we do ourselves. He knows us in our end, as well as from our beginning: he even knows us when we have forgotten ourselves. It seems to me that now, even when we look on the boy, we do so with eyes already once trained on the man we know as Benedict XVI. Not everyone will be comfortable with this, and if you are not, I ask you not to set much store by it.

To a small number of friends I owe gratitude for helpful suggestions and the correction of errors. Where mistakes persist, they are entirely mine. To: Robin Baird-Smith of Continuum Publishing, who had the idea for this book, and whose request to write it followed a homily I preached on Benedict XVI's election; and to Julian Chadwick, Ferdinand Knapp, Fr. Michael Lang *cong. orat.*, Susan Parsons, Fr. Andrew Wadsworth and Clare Watkins, each of whom read and commented on the book as it was being written. A few others kindly shared observations and reflections, and I am grateful to them. Thanks go also to Hal Broadbent, a research student at Heythrop, who provided the bibliography, at the end, of Benedict's works that are in English.

Wherever the book is deficient, for what has had to be left out, and if I have falsified or over-simplified, I ask forgiveness – of you, the reader, and of him about whom this book is written.

Laurence Paul Hemming
Feast of the Visitation of the
Blessed Virgin Mary 2005

ONE

Introduction

1

Habemus Papam!

The election of a new Pope is for the Church always joyful, although running hot on the heels of the sadness of the death of his predecessor. Decisive moments in history are rare – and yet rarer still that as they happen, millions of eyes are already trained in anticipation, watching them unfold. How tantalizing it was, as on 19 April 2005, we watched – the white smoke having gone up – on television screens around the world, for the appearance of the new pope at the balcony of St. Peter's Basilica. All cameras were trained on a window whose closed curtains rippled teasingly, yet to reveal what was taking place behind. One of the shortest conclaves in history had made a decisive choice.

Eventually the veil gave up its secret, and Cardinal Medina Estevez announced *habemus papam!* – 'we have a Pope'. The element of surprise was perhaps as much in the speed of the choice as in whom it was had been chosen: Joseph Cardinal Ratzinger, Pope Benedict XVI. Many who saw the new Pope emerge on the balcony that day speak of being captivated by his appearance – of his obvious gentleness and the joy with which he greeted the huge crowds in St. Peter's Square. Under his new white cassock could be seen clearly the sleeves, not of a black shirt but a jumper, worn to keep out the April cold of the Sistine Chapel, indicating after more than twenty years in Rome how 'Italian' this Bavarian had become. Certainly he was taken to the heart of the people of Rome immediately. Shortly after his election, Benedict thanked the Mayor of Rome for the warmth with which the Romans greeted him. Inhabitants of the city were not unused to seeing the former Cardinal on foot around the city, often in a black cassock and sporting a beret. On taking possession of his cathedral church as Bishop of Rome, the ancient basilica of St. John Lateran (the church in which the Pope has his *cathedra* or chair), he said 'as

Catholics we are all, in some way, also Romans!'

As Pope Benedict came blinking out into the April Roman sunlight, this book is written to ask: who is the man brought out before us? And what does he himself see as he comes out into the open? How are we to see him? And how will he see what lies before him: both the Catholic Church, of which he is now the Universal Pastor, and the world in which that Church stands forth and through which it makes its pilgrim way, a path that calls the world to its home in Jesus Christ, the Son of God? On discovering who had been elected, many rejoiced: some, indeed, expressed dismay. It seemed to many that the cardinals of the Catholic Church, pressed in secret conclave (which means literally under lock and key), had made a choice which would push the Church in an even more conservative direction than that supposedly taken by John Paul II (1978–2005). Commentators previously hostile to the recently deceased John Paul II suddenly discovered themselves full of fond nostalgia for his gentle reign. Those who seek in the

5

Church, and in the person of its shepherd, a policeman for the ills of the world could barely conceal their glee.

This book takes a very different view. I did indeed rejoice on hearing news of Benedict's election, but not because I want an arch-conservative pope who will police with an iron rod the morals of a wayward world. We live in a world that, especially in the past hundred years, has felt the iron of unwonted chastise-ment and far worse: Benedict XVI is well placed to know how that is true. He has called for dialogue and for openness in the debates that grip and sometimes tear the Church at the present time: he has also spoken of the present as a time of crisis in the life of the Church. In what follows I will explore both of those themes.

I was happy for three reasons: first, because the Church, bereaved of a cherished pastor, had once again been given a shepherd, one of formidable intellect and sensitivity; second, because the short conclave – barely twenty-four hours – had clearly been of a common, almost unanimous mind. In no sense could anyone claim that the cardinals were divided over whom to select for the most difficult and demanding role in the Church. If some faithful people might find it hard, at least initially, to understand the man chosen, nevertheless I was absolutely confident then (and am more so now) that the hearts of the great majority of Catholics will instinctively be strengthened by a choice that was at once definite in itself, and of one known to be so definite in his understanding of the Church; third, personally it meant all the more to me (as a theologian) that a man for whom theology means so much – a man steeped in the history, tradition and intellectual life of the Church – had been chosen for the See of Peter. It seemed most apt that a theologian should have been chosen to succeed a philosopher.

Benedict, in his first address, spoke of his surprise at being chosen as the Successor of Peter. It was well known that when (as he was required to do by canon law, the law of the Church) at seventy-five he submitted his resignation to John Paul II, that Benedict had really wanted to retire, to concentrate on writing in what he might have expected to be the quiet twilight of a life well and already fully lived. The choice of the name, Benedict, surprised us all. In his first general audience, before 15,000 people and just a week after his election, the Holy Father explained why he had chosen the name, and again spoke of his surprise at being chosen. He said 'I chose to call myself Benedict XVI ideally as a link to the venerated Pontiff, Benedict XV, who guided the Church through the turbulent times of the First World War' because, like Benedict XV (1914–1922) 'I place my ministry in the service of reconciliation and harmony between peoples, profoundly convinced that the great good of peace is above all a gift of God, a fragile and precious gift to be invoked, safeguarded and constructed, day after day and with everyone's contribution.'

To choose for his name the name of a pope outside the turbulence of the periods before and after the Second World War also suggests that this particular period, a period driven by extreme ideologies of far left and far right, is concluded. If Popes Pius XI (1922–1939) and

Pius XII (1939–1958) had steered the Church through the periods of Italian fascism and Nazi Germany, so the popes that succeeded them were forced to deal with the Soviet Union and the criminal régimes of Eastern Europe. John Paul II above all can claim to be the pope of the ending of the nightmare of the Marxist régimes of Europe. Could it be said, however, that to take a name in succession to the pope of the struggles of the First World War suggests that the forces that gave rise to that event – of European nihilism, of unbridled capitalism, of the instrumentalization of everything to economic processes and an almost infantile conception of the freedom of the human person, of at one and the same time a puerile optimism concerning man's capabilities and horizons and a dark negativity and cynicism over the human condition – are yet fully to be confronted and discerned?

The name Benedict – meaning 'one blessed of God' – recalls the Saint Benedict (*c.* 480–543) who is at once a patron of Europe (along with Saints Cyril [827–869] and Methodius [826–885], and St. Catherine of Siena [1347–1380]) and the father of Western monasticism as founder of the Benedictine Order of monks. Benedict, in explaining his choice of this name, reminded the audience that 'the progressive expansion of the Benedictine Order which he founded exercised an enormous influence on the spread of Christianity throughout the European continent'. The patron of Germany, sent by Gregory II to evangelize that land was St. Boniface (unknown–755) (an Englishman born in Devon at that), himself a Benedictine monk, and Benedict notes the devotion to St. Benedict in his native Bavaria.

There is a suggestion that the Pope also had in mind Benedict XIV (1740–1758) in choosing his own name, certainly, like Benedict XVI, a man of great scholarship. Benedict XIV corresponded with Voltaire (1694–1778). Voltaire said of this Benedict, in a way that might even be said of ours, 'I confess my surprise that our Holiness can so readily cite the verses of Virgil', indicating the way in which both Benedicts have been shaped not only deeply as Christians and Catholics, but also by all that is best in the history of European life. Not without significance, Benedict XIV urged caution in safeguarding the truth of the Faith from dilution in the work of evangelization, suggesting that this historical sense and education must yet redeem what has shaped it, and be fully Christian in its character.

2

Benedict, the Man and the Pope

No-one who has met Joseph Ratzinger, as a priest, a theologian, a cardinal, or as Pope Benedict XVI, has been left untouched by his own warmth, gentleness and unaffected charm. Those who have disagreed or clashed with him have remarked on these striking aspects of his personality, especially his openness. There is a school of thought that says that after a remarkable and lengthy papacy like that of Pope John Paul II's, a 'transitional' figure is often best chosen, an elder figure, likely to have a short reign and who can prepare the way for a younger and more vigorous successor. Benedict is seventy-eight, although Bavarians are a hardy lot and often long-lived. Of the length of a papal reign, no predictions can be made, but supposedly transitional figures can have a habit of surprising. Another of the most loved of recent popes, John XXIII (1958–1963), supposedly was elected as an intermediate figure between Pius XII (1939–1958) and the one thought to be his choice as successor, Giovanni Battista Montini, the future Pope Paul VI (1963–1978). He could not be elected on Pius XII's death because Pius XII had not yet made him a cardinal. John XXIII did make Montini a cardinal, and Montini did succeed him as Pope, but to an altogether different situation, after John XXIII had convened the Second Vatican Council.

Benedict XVI is perhaps two things, either one of which alone can often be found in men of the Church, but that only rarely come together in a single person. He is a remarkably accomplished academic theologian. He has written numerous works of theology, including an astonishing commentary on the Creed (the statement of faith sung or said by the whole congregation in every Catholic Church at the Mass of every ordinary Sunday of the Church's year) and published in English as *Introduction to Christianity*. Among his other theological accomplishments is a lengthy commentary on the Second Vatican Council, running to several volumes. More recently he has also continued to express strong and informed theological views through interviews with sympathetic journalists: in 1985 the Italian Vittorio Messori; and more latterly in 1996 and again in 2000 the southern German Peter Seewald (who became a Catholic after his initial encounters with Benedict).

Nevertheless what Benedict thinks runs against the common grain in many ways – here above all is a sign of the depth of his thought. As so often with men who do not think common thoughts, he has a capacity for sympathy for those even with whom he disagrees, and a willingness to enter dialogue: dialogue was a theme of Benedict's first address to the cardinal electors after the end of the conclave. Too often supposed respect for those who are different from us erases the basis for discussion and exchange – we avoid difficulties for fear of giving offence, and in falsely anticipating any offence we might give we do not even broach the difficulty. This is the mentality that eschews the joy of Christmas for fear of offending non-Christians. No such shallowness with Benedict, who has been unafraid to raise difficult and challenging matters in a spirit of conversation. There is a breadth and maturity in his approach to questions – especially difficult ones: his responses are never formulaic or doctrinaire. Often there is a wry humour in his replies. On being asked whether it were true that as a young man he was an enthusiast for reform in the Church, and if so, how could he reconcile that with his supposed conservatism as a cardinal, he replied to the effect that a man who is seventy should not seek to be a seventeen-year-old, nor the other way about.

One of the commentators on Benedict has remarked that 'most theologians also say that [his] thinking is largely derivative'. This judgement indicates the difficulty many have had in evaluating Benedict's theology. His thought is a deep confrontation with several things all at once: with the history of theological thinking from the earliest times; especially with the theology of the Second Vatican Council; and with kinds of thought that have arisen in theology in the contemporary situation (and this really means post-Second World War and the immediate pre-war period). Benedict's theology is anything but derivative, and is in fact a theology whose age is yet to come and may only now be dawning.

Most theologians, especially in the English-speaking nations, the very theologians to whom this commentator refers, have tended to regard theology as a speculative activity, an exercise in 'problem-solving', or one of reconciling modern trends in (especially scientific) thinking with theology. Too many theologians have taken the most superficial ways in which theological questions arise as their only possible form. Thus – let us say – after a great natural disaster or even a vicious atrocity to hear the cry 'where was God in this?' they hear this not as a plea for understanding from those gripped by the pain of tragedy and who are seeking to understand it, but rather as a factual statement of disbelief.

The refusal of Benedict to understand theology in these ways is what connects his theology with the second aspect of his person. For Benedict is a man of the most profound and direct piety. He has remarked that precisely in the very midst of the belief in progress and the increased faith in science, it is of great significance that 'the Church should have found herself represented most clearly in very simple people'. He says this in relation to St. Bernadette of Lourdes (1844–1879), but it could equally have been said about St. Catherine of Siena or many other transformative figures in the life and history of the Church. Benedict's theology is instinctively united to his faith, in a way many theologians struggle to achieve. For Benedict, theology amplifies and reflects on the experience of God given in faith. Theology investigates what believing *believes* – it is a servant discipline. It does not decide for or against either God or the Church or even the world. It amplifies and illuminates what is already occurring in the hearts of the faithful, as a result of the activity of God, who, as Trinity of persons, calls and sanctifies His people and redeems them. Where Benedict has questioned contemporary theology, it has been precisely in its dogmatism, in its contemporary tendency to systematize, and to inhibit or even destroy piety through its pursuit of an intellectual or historicist purity (and here is the pretension to the speculative) which does not lead the believing heart into a deeper love of God. Benedict, the supposed dogmatist, in fact has stood against these kinds of dogmatism in ways on which we will touch as we proceed.

New popes, if they have not worked in the Vatican, can take up to two years to 'find their way around', to establish and stamp their personal authority on the Curia – the complex of offices and bureaux that make up the Church's day to day machinery. Benedict, as one who headed the most senior of the curial offices, the Congregation for the Doctrine of the Faith for more than twenty years, knows the inside working of the Vatican intimately, and perhaps not just the face it displays to its head, the Pope.

The appointment of Archbishop William Levada from the Archdiocese of San Francisco as the Pope's successor as Prefect of the

Congregation for the Doctrine of the Faith (often known simply as 'CDF') suggests two important things in this regard. First, many North Americans will be delighted by the appointment of an American to the most senior role in the Church any of their countrymen has held; but the second reason is perhaps less obvious. Archbishop Levada worked in the Congregation for the Doctrine of the Faith as an official between 1976 and 1982, and has continued to have some involvement with the Congregation in the years since, especially during his time in San Francisco. As the new Pope is, at least in form, familiar with the working of the office of the papacy, so Levada will be familiar with the working of his Congregation. Moreover, he will have overlapped briefly with the new Pope as he was beginning his Prefecture in 1981: he will be familiar, at least to an extent, with the working methods not just of the Congregation but also of its former Prefect. He will perhaps have less to learn than many other potential successors. Levada, an academic, although not with the breadth of experience of his predecessor (having been a diocesan bishop for a number of years), has been appointed at just under sixty-nine, and will have just a few years before he is in any case (under canon law) required to tender his resignation. The chances are, therefore, that he will not survive the current papacy in office.

As former Archbishop of San Francisco, Levada is familiar with the situation in which the Church finds herself in the West. He has proved himself adept at reconciling Catholic teaching with the demands of secular life, and sensitive in the questions that manifest themselves in the complexities of city life, especially in the United States – the economy and nation that is driving the attitudes and outlook that arise from its immense economic prosperity. If prosperity drives many of these questions, it is a wealth that is far from being equally distributed even in the West, let alone across the globe.

There are, therefore, clear signs that Benedict will stamp his own personality on the Curia with speed. There are also signs that he will exercise a more direct and personal authority than his predecessor.

This book is intended for those curious to know a little about the man Joseph Ratzinger, but perhaps more curious to know a little about what and how he thinks. I will give some biographical background; perhaps as I proceed just a little background to some of the controversies that have shaped his reputation – for ill or good. More than anything, this book seeks to introduce a general reader to the themes that have marked his writing and thinking that are likely to have a bearing on the character and style of this papacy, and which give strong indicators for how he will act as Pope, and why. For reasons I will endeavour to explain as we proceed, there are just a handful of themes that I believe are of central importance as a key to both the office and the man.

TWO

The Man

3

An Introduction and Early Life

Joseph Ratzinger was born on 16 April 1927 in the tiny town of Marktl am Inn in southern Bavaria (almost on the Austrian border), which that year was Holy Saturday, the day between Good Friday and Easter Day. The theologian Hans Urs von Balthasar (1905–1988), made a cardinal by John Paul II (but dying just before receiving his cardinal's 'hat'), and a friend and collaborator of Bene-dict's from the time of their first meeting in Bonn when Benedict taught there, has made much of the significance of this day. Holy Saturday is the day between days, the day when we await in hope but do not yet experience the full glory of the resurrection, the time in which each Christian is called to live – it is the very condition of faith. In those days the Church celebrated the first part of the Easter Liturgy, the Liturgy of

the Resurrection, on this morning, and so the
newly born Joseph was immediately baptized
in the font blessed in the course of the splen-
did Easter liturgy for that day. Benedict has
himself said of this event: 'To be the first person baptized with the new water was seen as a
sig-nificant act of Providence. I have always
been filled with thanksgiving for having had
my life immersed in this way in the Easter
Mystery.'

The Germany of 1927 was in turmoil, in
ways hard to understand in the comparative
prosperity and political stability of the modern West. Rarely is it acknowledged that the First
World War did not end so much because the
Allied Forces 'defeated' the Kaiser, as because
there was mass mutiny on both sides in the
army, and in Germany in the navy as well. A
revolutionary fervour was abroad – partially
inspired by the Bolshevik revolution in Russia
in 1917, but more because of the vast forces
unleashed through the rapid industrialization
of a country barely sixty years in existence.
Bavaria, rural, perhaps by the standards of
more industrialized centres even 'backward'

(compared to its contemporary industrial pre-eminence), briefly declared itself a socialist republic for just a few months in 1919, and on the collapse of that endeavour many were simply rounded up and shot. Continuing unemployment, industrial and social unrest fomented from the far left and far right, the instability and then spectacular collapse of the currency, polarized German society from top to bottom, and all conspired to destroy the tranquillity of daily life. The 'Weimar' republic (1919–1933) lacked either the political will or the popular confidence to resolve these difficulties, in the face of crippling war reparations exacted by the supposed victors. It was in this context that Hitler and Nazism gained first a foothold from the late 1920s up to the elections in 1930, and then power in 1933. Democratic opposition to Nazism persisted longest in Bavaria, largely because of the existence and activity of the *Zentrumspartei*, the Catholic 'Centre Party' which was the last democratic party to be disbanded after the Nazis came to power, largely in the wake of the Concordat between the Vatican and Hitler in 1933.

Precisely because of the strength of the Catholic Church in Bavaria, Hitlerism found it harder to gain popularity in Bavaria than anywhere else in Germany. As is well known, the Nazis from the outset ruled through terror and the violence of their street-thugs, especially early on, with the 'SA' storm-troops. We are now familiar with the hideous persecution of Jews in Nazi Germany, beginning with the racial laws enacted on the Nazis coming to power, and ending with the systematic slaughter of millions in the death-camps. Perhaps less well understood is the fury unleashed on the Catholic Church, who, after the socialists and trade unionists arrested on Hitler's accession, were second in line to excite Hitler's wrath. Alongside the millions of Jews and others selected on racial grounds for mechanized murder, thousands of priests, religious (monks and nuns) and lay Catholics also died at Nazi hands. Opposition of any kind was met with decisive, often fatal, consequences.

Fuller details of Benedict's youth have been published elsewhere and I do not intend to dwell on them, but one issue remains important to understand the mentality of the present Pope. It is worth remembering that Benedict was born into the midst of these convulsions, among the most violent of the tensions of the working out of the chaos that was much of the Europe of the early twentieth century, and neither he nor his family were left untouched by them. Benedict has been aware from his earliest youth of the struggles that have worked themselves out first in Europe and then in nation after nation in consequence of the dramatic effects of industrialization and social and economic upheaval. The outlook of the present Pope has been decisively shaped, and from within, by some of the most terrible events in European history.

His father, also called Joseph, was a policeman, unafraid on occasion to criticize the new Nazi rulers, even before they came fully to power. For this reason the family was forced to move not once, but several times, in Benedict's earliest years, in order to escape the wrath of Nazi officials. In 1932 the elder Joseph Ratzinger's outspoken criticisms of local Nazis forced the family's relocation to the town of Aschau am Inn under the Alps. In 1937 they moved to Hufschlag, on the outskirts of the comparatively larger town of Traunstein, where the young Joseph as a teenager excelled academically and was able to attend the local *Gymnasium* or High School. The German education system was up to that time one of the finest in the world. Classical languages – Latin and Greek – then formed the basis of a good German education, together with a good understanding of the civilizations that spoke them. Benedict has himself spoken of the importance of the education he received, commenting that 'an education in Greek and Latin antiquity created a mental attitude that resisted seduction by a totalitarian ideology'. Already the Nazis had begun to interfere with this curriculum and he notes with immense relief that it affected, not so much him, but mainly those in the years below him. This classical education has stood him in great stead in his later theological study: he has read closely not only the ancient writers of the Church – the Fathers – who wrote in Latin, but also those, like Maximus the Confessor (580–662), who wrote in Greek.

Benedict, having been elected Pope, gave his acceptance address to the Conclave in Latin. That anyone should do such a thing may seem strange in a world that routinely thinks of Latin as a 'dead language'. No-one should underestimate the importance of Latin (and Greek), for either the history or the records and study of theology of the Church, and (arguably more important yet) for the history of Europe itself. For most of European history Latin and Greek have been the languages of intellectual energy and commerce. They constitute the memory of the Church and of this continent: to lose your memory – which is the same as to lose access to what it contains – is to lose your knowledge of who you are and where you have come from. Of course the 'memory' exists in translations: anyone who has translated something from one language into another knows what a precarious business it is. Much enters the process of translation even despite our best efforts to keep faithfully to the original text. The outcry over the crude (because so hastily produced) translations of the Mass when it came fully into the vernacular is a reminder of this fact. Translations inevitably date and go stale, while texts in their original language have a habit of retaining their pristine freshness.

In 1939 Benedict had entered, in the footsteps of his older brother, the junior seminary – the first steps on the road to priesthood in the Catholic Church. The teenage Joseph Ratzinger managed to evade nearly all the requirements of the Nazi régime, of (compulsory) attendance at Hitler Youth meetings and, even as the nation decayed into chaos, of anything more than temporary involvement in the 'Third Reich's' maniacal efforts at self-defence as the whole country disintegrated. In 1997 Benedict commented that his brother had been forced to join the Hitler Youth, which he had nothing to do with until he was also forced to join when he entered the seminary, 'but as soon as I left the seminary, I never went to see them again'. This caused him real hardship, because in order to achieve certain things or get a reduced tuition fee 'one had to prove one was a member of the Hitler Youth'. Not even for the sake of a mere certificate would the young Benedict attend meetings. Eventually a teacher – who was in fact himself a Nazi – gave him the certificate without him having to attend.

For a year or so Benedict was required to assist in the anti-aircraft corps. Briefly, in 1944, having come of age for labour service, he was drafted first for labour service and then, as the war in Germany ended, into the infantry, although a combination of question-able health and the collapse of the army meant little was required of him until finally he deserted and went home, narrowly escaping summary execution in an encounter with some SS troopers on the way (the SS had orders to kill suspected deserters). After Germany's surrender, and under the French occupying forces briefly a prisoner of war, he was finally released to his family in July 1945. Once again, Benedict's first-hand experience of the destructive effects of political tyranny and collapse cannot be stressed too strongly. He has understood from the inside (and

instinctively resisted from the first) Nazi political ideology, especially for its inhumanity and
dogmatism. His later instinctual opposition to
Marxism, which broke in on the Western stage
especially in the universities from 1968 on-
wards, is perhaps not so much motivated (as
some commentators have suggested) by a professorial disdain for the thuggishness of ideal-
istic left-wing students, as by an understanding
of what ideological extremism can result in
and where it had already led in his youth.

In November 1945 Benedict, again with his
brother, resumed study in the seminary at
Freising, and in 1947 proceeded to theological
studies in the University of Munich, although
the actual buildings in Munich were for a
while unusable and so initially he lived and
studied at a former hunting lodge at Fürsten-
ried, to the south of Munich. This was a happy
time, marked by a close sense of collegiality
with fellow students that could never quite be
recovered once the faculty relocated to the city
itself, still very much damaged after the war.

On the feast of Saints Peter and Paul both
Joseph and Georg Ratzinger were ordained

priest by Cardinal Faulhaber (1869–1952) in the Cathedral at Freising, followed by immensely happy celebrations for both young priests in their home church of St. Oswald in Traunstein. Discussing this, Benedict notes something about the life of faith that I have repeatedly found to be true. He notes in the joy of the festivities around his and his brother's ordination and First Mass (always a great occasion in Catholic Bavaria) that human friendship could arise almost spontaneously 'precisely because we ourselves were not the point'.

4

The Doctoral Student and work for the *Habilitation*

Benedict began his higher studies – he suggests – almost by accident, and shortly before his ordination to the priesthood. In the theology faculty associated with the University of Munich where he had been conducting his studies for priesthood, the Herzogliches Georgianum, there was a custom whereby a different member of the faculty each year would set a topic for a prize assignment. Candidates were then invited to submit a thesis within nine months, anonymously, and if they achieved the prize, they were effectively accepted for doctoral study, with the assignment counting as a major component of the doctorate. A professor well known to Benedict, Gottlieb Söhngen (1892–1971), indicated that he was setting the title of the prize assignment for that year as 'The People and House of God in Augustine's Doctrine of the Church'. Clearly Söhngen had recognized Benedict's abilities as a potential theologian and wanted to encourage him on to a doctorate.

It is not all that uncommon for study for the priesthood to conclude with study for a higher degree, and to be accepted for this study almost certainly indicated then, as it would now, a life of teaching – perhaps at seminary level, perhaps in a university faculty. It is more common in the continental European system for the subject for a doctorate to be given to a student, rather than for him to choose it for himself. Nevertheless, the subject was in this case well-chosen. Benedict has often indicated his sympathy for the theology of St. Augustine (354–430). St. Augustine is one of the finest minds the Western Church has ever known, and he has left behind him a vast collection of works. Among the best known of his writings is his *City of God*, as well as numerous commentaries on Scripture, especially the psalms.

At the same time as he began to study for his doctorate, Benedict began to read Henri de

Lubac (1896–1991). De Lubac, eventually to be made a cardinal by John Paul II for his extraordinary contribution to theology, was transforming the approach of Catholic theology to the Church Fathers. His important work *Corpus Mysticum*, which Benedict read at this time, represents a fundamental engagement with the Church Fathers of East and West on a scale arguably not known in the Catholic Church since Newman (1801–1890). Moreover Newman's engagement with the Fathers had begun when he was an Anglican, although his reading of them is above all what led him to become a Catholic. De Lubac had struggled to have his understanding of the Fathers accepted in the Church – and had even been under some suspicion for the theological understanding he had developed. Benedict describes de Lubac's work as 'the dramatic struggle of French Catholicism for a new penetration of the faith into the intellectual life of our time'.

From the very beginning of Benedict's intellectual formation we can see the emergence of what was to become and remain a focal concern of the Church, up to the Second

Vatican Council and beyond it to the present day – the way in which the Church addresses the wider societies, and indeed the age she finds herself located within. This has been a concern of Benedict's from the beginning of his serious theological work, a pressing concern that without doubt arises from the struggles he witnessed in the Germany of his youth – the struggles of the Church to both come to terms with and survive Nazi terror, and which will have attuned him to the relation between the life of faith and social and political questions. Mature answers to these questions are almost always ground out of the anguished place of public exchange and debate – they do not originate in, and only tangentially belong to, the lecture room.

In de Lubac's work *Catholicism*, Benedict detected 'a quiet debate with both liberalism and Marxism'. What Benedict perceived in de Lubac and his thought was the desire to address the questions of the day with an outlook shaped by the Church's own tradition of understanding (rather than methods of understanding derived from secular life), exemplified by the

Church Fathers, the very figures who had given continuing shape to that tradition. Where this influence was transformative for Benedict is that he saw that what de Lubac was arguing for was not a merely individualistic concern with personal salvation. This was a perspective that had been strongly emphasized in the wake of the upheavals of the nineteenth century, especially in the Catholic Church's struggles with political liberalism (struggles which, after all, had briefly resulted in Pope Pius IX [1846–1878] being exiled from Rome in 1849 until the following year). De Lubac also emphasized the social context within which that salvation is offered and proclaimed. This did indeed represent a profound shift in the Catholic theology of the time, which to some extent – because of the controversies over Modernism since Pius X (1903–1914) and with the emphasis on a certain kind of study of St. Thomas Aquinas (c. 1225–1274) (so-called 'neo-Thomism') – had made Catholic theology somewhat individualistic, formulaic, and even inward-looking (in ways that have odd parallels with some of the situation of

Catholic theology today). It was de Lubac's invigorating influence that fed Benedict's emerging theological mind, and he won the prize, proceeding to doctoral study. Benedict's doctorate was awarded in 1953.

In order to hold a chair at a university in Germany (as indeed in Poland) even today, there is after doctoral study a period of study for a second thesis, known as a *Habilitation*. Those working for a *Habilitation* have much more choice over the topic of the thesis than in their doctorates, and the *Habilitation* thesis is much more demanding than a doctorate. Benedict was advised by Söhngen, the professor who had seen him through his doctorate, to study a mediaeval theologian, and he chose the Franciscan, St. Bonaventure (1221–1274). A lot has been made of Benedict's sympathy for Augustine and choice of Bonaventure, and not therefore Bonaventure's almost exact (and more famous) contemporary, St. Thomas Aquinas. Aquinas was certainly widely studied at the time, and his theology had been given a special prominence in the Church by Pope Leo XIII's (1878–1903) Encyclical Letter *Aeterni*

Patris of 1879. The way in which St. Thomas was studied at that time was, however, more rigid in a way that contemporary study of him is not. It is almost possible to say that since Vatican II Aquinas has been rediscovered in an entirely new way, and the extraordinary richness of his theology has become much more available now than it was then. If Benedict was not drawn to St. Thomas at that time, he has since noted that 'St. Thomas Aquinas is both a theologian who opens the door to a new vision of theology, with the integration of Aristotelian thought, and at the same time a perfectly patristic theologian'.

I propose to discuss one aspect of Benedict's *Habilitation* thesis later on, but, as can sometimes happen with the examination of theses in university life (and precisely because Benedict's work was profoundly influenced by some of the most recent thought of its day) his *Habilitation* found itself in some trouble. The thesis was submitted for examination and approval, and after a long delay it was rejected. Although it had been directed by Söhngen, it was (as is customary) examined by a board of examiners of whom the leading dogmatic theologian Michael Schmaus (1897–1992) was one, and he objected to key elements of what Benedict had written. Benedict himself notes that the study of medi-aeval theology in Munich had not advanced beyond its pre-war state and, as he says, 'the great new breakthroughs that had been made in the meantime, particularly by those writing in French, had not even been acknowledged'. In the turmoil of Europe immediately after the war this is hardly surprising. De Lubac himself is said to have carried his card-index of patris-tic references around in his pockets during the war, and many books either were published in only a partial state in the 1940s (to be pub-lished in proper editions later), or even – by 1943 until years later – could not be published at all. This was either because of acute paper shortages or worse (in Germany especially), because of interference and even censorship from the authorities. The years after the war were often preoccupied with rebuilding shat-tered faculties, and with digesting large num-bers of students, many former combatants, whose studies had been delayed or interrupted by war itself, by imprisonment, and by displacement. There was little time for some professors to catch up with the latest developments in their fields.

It is precisely at times like these – times of extreme turmoil – that scholarly questions are sharpened. The scholarly question of the relation between faith and society could not have received more sharpening at this time, when the sound of exploding ordnance had barely faded into echo, and when the trauma of war and disintegration of the state was succeeded by occupation by foreign powers (in Germany) and social and political upheaval and reconstruction. This is the time when the cry goes up: 'where is God in all of this?' At precisely the time questions like these are posed, the resources to respond to them adequately are stretched to the limit or even exhausted. Some thinkers move into the vanguard quickly, with energy for the questions at hand; others lag behind or consciously take up the rear, seeing the urgent need for reconstruction and continuity, not innovation or improvisation; others simply have neither time nor spare energy to stay abreast of developments. The younger and less experienced the mind, the more likely it will be swayed by the vagaries of the moment. Benedict comments on the arguments in his thesis that 'with a forthrightness not advisable in a beginner, I criticized the superseded positions'. We can hear in this remark both a humility before what came as a considerable shock, and also the verve he had for the questions at hand. Benedict is hardly alone if as a young scholar his passion for a renewed approach to questions led him to intemperate judgements, to the distaste of his examiners.

The *Habilitation* could have been failed outright, ending all hopes for an academic future, but in fact Benedict was given the opportunity to rewrite it, and noticing where the examiners had been least critical, he went on from those sections to develop a successful thesis from the ruins. He was duly awarded the title, and the right to teach and hold a chair in theology, in 1957. Events like these in a young scholar's life can be humiliating to the point of devastation – even when the thesis eventually succeeds. It is worth saying that the very best and most competent theses can get into the worst trouble: the lessons gained, especially for a forthright and powerful mind used to excelling, can be of incalculable value. As we know from comments he has made later, Benedict took the experience to heart and has himself taken care to understand the plight of others in the course of being examined.

5

The University Professor

Benedict taught as a *Privatdozent* – literally, a
'private lecturer' in the University of Munich
only briefly, for less than a year. A position like
this is in Germany only semi-official, and the
teacher has no salary, receiving support for the
actual teaching he does. Within a year – on
1 January 1958, he was given his first chair of
Fundamental Theology and Dogma at the
College of Philosophy and Theology at Freising.
Within months he was offered a more presti-
gious chair in Fundamental Theology in Bonn,
and he began teaching there in April 1959,
with consequences we will discuss later for
Benedict's extensive involvement in the Second
Vatican Council. Bonn began with great hap-
piness for Benedict, marred shortly afterwards
by the death of his father.

In 1962 the dogmatic theologian Hermann

Volk (1903–1988) was made bishop of the
ancient See of Mainz, and, having befriended
Benedict, Volk pressed Benedict to be his
replacement at his former chair of Dogmatic
Theology in Münster. This represented a somewhat different turn for Benedict in his own
theological work. Hitherto Benedict had spe-
cialized in Fundamental Theology. Dogma is a
related discipline, and Benedict was well
qualified to teach either. In English-speaking
contexts, especially in secular departments of
theology (but even in many Catholic faculties
in America) these two disciplines are not really
distinguished, but go under the heading of
systematic theology. In fact they are very different. Fundamental Theology is much more
closely related to philosophy, especially the
kind of 'Catholic philosophy' taught in some
American or French universities. Dogmatic
Theology is the specific study of the doctrines
of the Church. Many of these require a good
knowledge of philosophy to be understood well,
but Dogmatics is not taught philosophically,
above all because the justification or ground
for dogmas is not philosophical. The dogmas

of the Church are true because they have been revealed to be true by the activity of God, as discerned through his Church. Dogmatic Theology would for that reason have drawn on Benedict's study of both sacred Scripture and the Church Fathers, much more so than he would have required in Fundamental Theology.

Initially Benedict declined the offer from Münster, only to accept and begin work there in the summer of 1963. Again a new appointment was followed within months by a death, this time of Benedict's mother, in December. In his remarks on this we get a glimpse of what motivates his understanding of the way in which faith can transform a human person: 'I know of no more convincing proof for the faith than precisely the pure and unalloyed humanity that the faith allowed to mature in my parents.'

In 1966 Benedict was invited to a chair in Dogmatic Theology at the University of Tübingen: this was Tübingen's second invitation – the first had come in 1959. Unlike British or American theology faculties, faculties of theology in Germany are, although state-funded, nevertheless confessional. Traditionally they have been either Catholic or reformed (belonging to one of the Evangelische Kirche provinces or *Länder*). Tübingen is unusual because not only is it the foremost faculty of theology in Germany, it also has both Catholic and reformed faculties of theology. To be invited to a chair there would be regarded by many as the pinnacle of a career. The theologian Hans Küng (1928–), with whom Benedict had already had contact, strongly supported Benedict's appointment, although the warmth between them was not to last.

Benedict's arrival in Tübingen coincided with the wave of student radicalism that swept through Western Europe and had repercussions even behind the Berlin Wall, above all in Czechoslovakia. Benedict himself notes that 'while until now Bultmann's [1884–1976] theology and Heidegger's philosophy had determined the frame of reference for thinking' (and much of Bultmann's theology was influenced by a somewhat one-sided interpretation of Heidegger [1889–1976]) the existentialist mood in the universities collapsed, to be replaced by Marxism. Ernst Bloch (1885–1977), also teaching in Tübingen, came to the fore. Benedict comments that the consequence of the Marxist fervour that swept through Europe and manifested itself in Tübingen was that Marxism retained biblical hope as its basis, but, as Benedict notes 'inverted it by keeping the religious ardour but eliminating God and replacing him with the political activity of man'.

Not for the first time was Benedict confronted with the perversion of the religious into the political. He notes in his memoirs how much Nazi activity had a liturgical aspect to it. One only has to witness Leni von Riefenstahl's cinematic representations of the Nazi party congresses of 1933 and 1935 to see how liturgy can be turned to political ends. Here again aspects of religious faith – fervour, anticipation of a kingdom yet to come, concern for the dispossessed – were transformed for ideological ends. The description Benedict gives to the activity of the students in this time could equally have applied to the Germany of the 1930s – 'the frightful face of this atheistic piety ... its psychological terror, the abandon with which every moral consideration could be overthrown as a bourgeois residue'. There is not one item in this list that did not also form part of the Nazi and fascist programmes of the pre-war period. What Benedict identifies is the connection between political ideology and the instrumentalization of means to ends that characterized ideologies of extreme left and right in these two periods, and, indeed, still drives in many ways the (supposedly centrist) contemporary political and economic outlook. Simply labelling a position as democratic – or even moderate – does not free it from the desire to manipulate everything without regard to the truth.

Benedict did not remain long in Tübingen, but had the opportunity to return to his native Bavaria. In 1967 the Bavarian government (Bavaria still calls itself a 'Free State', a concession from Bismarck on becoming united with Germany in the nineteenth century) opened a new university in the ancient city of Regensburg, and in 1969, after several invitations, Benedict agreed to come to a chair in

Dogmatic Theology. A move of this kind is unusual – to go from one of the leading faculties in his subject in the world to a new provincial university with the varnish barely dry on its doors is strange. Benedict was hardly withdrawing, however, for he had established himself as an important voice at the deliberations surrounding the Second Vatican Council, and had been appointed by Pope Paul VI to the new International Theological Commission which followed on the heels of the Council. It was at this point that his friendship with the remarkable theologian Hans Urs von Balthasar became cemented, as did friendship with the figure who had so influenced his intellectual development, Henri de Lubac. Of these he says 'never again have I found anyone with such a comprehensive theological and humanistic education as Balthasar and de Lubac'.

Benedict spent eight years in Regensburg – eight years which saw his participation in the international theological journal founded in the wake of Vatican II, *Concilium*. As he, de Lubac, von Balthasar and Karl Lehmann

(1936–) diverged from what they saw as the false optimism of the theology represented by that journal, they founded the journal *Communio*. Lehmann was then teaching Dogmatic Theology in Freiburg, and was later to replace Volk as bishop of Mainz in 1983 (Lehmann was to become a cardinal in 2001 – his name being added to the consistory a week later than the others announced). Lehmann is a figure of extraordinary intellectual influence and popularity in Germany – he has even been the subject of an advert for a national newspaper, the *Frankfurter Allgemeine Zeitung*. Also significant in the conversations around the foundation of *Communio* was the founder of the Milanese 'Comunione e Liberazione' movement, Luigi Giussani (1922–2005), at whose funeral Benedict was to officiate shortly before becoming Pope.

Benedict's growing international reputation meant that he drew energetic young doctoral students toward him, many from outside Germany. Among the best known have been the American Jesuit Joseph Fessio and Irish priest Vincent Twomey. What was the significance of

Benedict's move to Regensburg? I think it less likely that he moved because of a professorial distaste for student radicalism, than the surer knowledge that for him a genuine theological vision, the product of long and careful reflection, could not be developed in a large and tempestuous faculty. Had such a prominent position (as at Tübingen) simply come too early? Benedict says himself 'the feeling of acquiring a theological vision that was ever more clearly my own was the most wonderful experience of the Regensburg years'. Regensburg also reunited him with his family: he shared a house with his sister – his brother, directing the Cathedral Choir of the city, always being close by.

6

Fellow Worker for the Truth

In 1977, after a distinguished career as a university teacher spanning almost twenty years and four universities, Benedict was named Archbishop of Munich and Freising, the diocese for which he had originally been ordained. The legend that Pope Benedict took for his episcopal coat of arms was *cooperatores veritatis*. Literally translated it means 'fellow worker for the truth'. The phrase comes from the beginning of the first letter of St. John the Apostle. St. John speaks of how in supporting our Christian brethren, we earnestly hope that we might become fellow workers in the truth. To labour for the truth means that we should become co-workers of Christ, he who described himself as 'the Way, the Truth and the Life'. A fellow worker for the truth is one who makes the truth that Jesus Christ *is* manifest and visible in the world, and so brings it out of hiding into the light of the day. To labour in this truth and to co-operate with it is to lead the world home to the one in whom it was created and through whom it has been redeemed. The legend 'fellow worker for the truth' is therefore a most apt description of a bishop: whether bishop of a diocese; or working in a Vatican dicastery; or as Bishop of Rome. The Pope has, in commenting on this phrase, noted how appropriate it is, not just for a bishop, but also how it defines the work of a theologian. One could almost say, in that one of the specific gifts of a bishop is to teach the truth, this phrase unites his two vocations of bishop and theologian and makes them one because it indicates the need always to be seeking the truth.

The word for truth in the Greek of the New Testament, and in the philosophy of the ancient writers, literally means un-hiding. Truth is a disclosure. It has a sense of some thing not yet known being drawn out from its hiddenness and brought into view: unveiling. In the contemporary West especially, we have come to embrace an understanding of truth as self-evidence. What we can see most plainly, we are most apt to believe is true. Encapsulated in this is the modern appeal to personal experience. Because I feel it, and all the more because I feel it keenly, it must be true (whatever 'it' is). If you cannot see what I most earnestly feel, you must be blind – or blinded by some covert commitment to power that even you are not fully aware of yourself. This understanding of truth has its roots in the declaration of René Descartes (1596–1650), the founder of modern philosophy, that he would prove the existence of God to be more certain than the truths of mathematics. That millions doubt the fact of God shows his proof, and all proofs of this kind, fail. That reason, to be true, must always be self-evident has corrupted the meaning of reason. For if it is certainly true that two plus two equals four, and if we have striven to make every kind of truth conform to something like this, we who know that two plus two equals four have often forgotten *why*. There is a 'why', a proper explanation of why two and two is four. One not less than Plato (427–*c*. 347 BC) said that any fool could count, few understood *why* they could, and the path in to the 'why' of truth (and there are many kinds of truth) is not easy nor at all self-evident. There is a 'why' to counting (and I do not intend to trouble you with it now, although Plato knew it well), but *that* there is reminds us that in the West especially we have forgotten that truth is attained – especially in the public sphere – through careful deliberation, and its results are precarious and precious. The results of truth and its deliberations have to be attained with discipline and rigour, guarded when attained, and handed on to future generations with the utmost care. Reason is not the steps in a proof, but the means by which we deliberate, and through which we come to a knowledge of the truth.

This does not make the truth relative, or provisional, or dependent on opinion. Few truths are as simple as 'two plus two equals four'. The result of 'two plus two' is not in any way provisional – we can be certain of it. But the 'why' is difficult, both to understand, and keep ahead of us. Moreover, the 'why' is not needed in every actual calculation, which is why it has often been forgotten. 'Two plus two equals four' is therefore true, but only *part* of the truth of what counting is and why it is possible. Most truth, especially that arrived at in the public sphere, is marked by an incompleteness. Here we must make a distinction between truth as it is discovered philosophically, and theological truth. Philosophical (and scientific) truth often has a provisional, contingent, aspect to it. St. Thomas Aquinas once reminded his readers that very often when we thought we had arrived at the essential truth of a thing, we were still often deceived, and knew only its appearances, and so what the truth *seemed* to be. The truth revealed by God, however, is higher than the truth given in philosophy, and more certain, more to be trusted. Of course, as St. Thomas himself said, even this truth will only be confirmed at the end of time, when all will be revealed by God in its entirety. One of the questions Pope Benedict has meditated on profoundly is how we come to know this higher truth of faith – a truth that otherwise goes by the name of revelation.

To know revealed truth is also not a simple matter. Many of those who rejoiced in the election of Pope Benedict have done so because – as I suggested earlier – they have also fallen for the journalistic picture of him as an inquisitor and enforcer. These are the ones who want the Church to act as a – most often as a moral – policeman for the world's ills. Among them there is much talk of 'natural law'. As one of these 'moral conservatives' put it to me recently, 'the law of God is written in our hearts'. But just as those who have been shocked by the thought of Benedict the enforcer's election have been taken in by a journalistic caricature, so those who have revelled in it have also been taken in. For Benedict himself knows well that God's law is something we have to come to discover, not first in our hearts, but primarily in the person of Christ. Our hearts are wayward; as men and women we are marked by the effects of original sin, which obscures our access to the perfect law of God. If this law was once written in our hearts, it is now defaced and only partially known – we have to rediscover the full truth of it by other means. The question is *how* this discovery takes place, and the answer to this question turns on the means by which God reveals himself. In answering this question it will become clear that the Church acts not as a policeman, but a doctor – one who provides medicine for sin and for the overcoming of its effects.

Above all, the truth that is revealed in the person of Jesus Christ reminds us that the highest truths and highest Truth itself are made manifest personally. The way to the Father is through the Son, in the life of the Spirit. When we understand that truth is disclosed through deliberation, through reserve (the constant reminding myself I could be wrong, and checking myself along the way), and through contemplation of the things that are higher, we realize that truth is not often given all at once and in a rush, but over time and even over history itself.

7

The Cardinal Prefect

Benedict was appointed Cardinal Prefect of the Congregation for the Doctrine of the Faith by Pope John Paul II in November 1981. He was Prefect for nearly twenty-four years, during some of the greatest turbulence that the Catholic Church has ever known within her own precincts. Appointed just four years after becoming a diocesan bishop, Benedict held this job for almost the full length of the previous papacy. It is unusual to have a man of Benedict's formidable intellect in the role – the Prefects of the Congregation have by tradition been solid, rather than outstanding, theologians, whose primary role has been more managerial than professorial. Times of change are also times of danger: it should be added, danger is not something always to be shied away from. It is in danger that courage is most

visible. If the Second Vatican Council represented the most serious attempt by the
Catholic Church to engage with the modern
world, it is unsurprising that the engagement
began within the Church even before it has
begun with the world. Much of the controversy
of the post-conciliar period has been a period of
painful and awkward discovery – discovering
just how much a part of the contemporary
world the Church really is, and how much a
prey we are to the way the world thinks and
acts. The Church, as St. Benedict's *Rule* suggests,
is a school for sinners, a school of the Lord's
service. Only as that has become clear has it
been possible to understand how the Church
might address a world of which she is so much
an intimate part.

The Congregation for the Doctrine of the
Faith is the most senior of the organs (often
referred to by their proper title of dicasteries)
of the Vatican Curia. In the Athens of ancient
Greece a Dicast was pretty much what we
would know as a magistrate or district judge: a
dicastery was his magisterial court. The dicasteries of the Roman Curia – the Vatican – are

much like courts with an executive office or bureau attached. Headed by a cardinal, they consist of other cardinals who sit together in plenary session from time to time, with a small number of subordinate officials to support them. It is often presumed the Vatican is awash with minor officials who manage the business of the dicasteries in between their plenary sessions. This is in fact anything but the case. The dicasteries each (at most) consist in a handful of men and sometimes now women too: one or two bishops and a few priests, perhaps one or two women religious.

Much is made of the fact that the Congregation for the Doctrine of the Faith is the descendant of the 'Office of the Roman Inquisition' and until recently went under the name of the Holy Office – so that its erstwhile Prefect has often been referred to by commentators as an inquisitor or enforcer. The role of the Congregation is not inquisitorial: it is primarily advisory, a safeguard, to ensure that the highest and most careful consideration is given to doctrinal questions, especially where there is dispute, or where a lack of clarity can lead to confusion in the hearts of the faithful. Occasionally, and then dramatically, the Congregation has intervened to decide specific questions or cases. Quite why and quite what is at stake I hope will become clear as this little book unfolds. I have already suggested that theology is not and can never be a primarily speculative affair. Theology as a discipline (a discipline of whom the guardians are, properly speaking, the bishops – sometimes referred to as the Pastors – of the Church) is an aid and support to faith, above all, the faith of the ordinary Christian.

Strictly speaking, theologians who are not themselves bishops share in the office and duty of the bishops to teach the faith: as such the relation to the bishops is one of obedience. Obedience here does not mean blind or slavish repetition of the bishops' opinions. Obedience means unity of intention and spirit with the Church's Pastors, for the sake of the holiness of the faithful. The bishops are the ones who have by right and as part of their office the duty to teach. When they teach, they do so in unity and communion with the Pope – and this unity of intention and will is itself the 'Ordinary Magisterium' of the Church's activity of teaching. Here then is a way to understand the Church – a way that John Paul II had once stressed when he said that 'it is to the holiness of the faithful that the hierarchical structure of the Church is totally ordered'. There need be no doubt that this is Benedict's understanding as well – indeed his solicitude for the ordinary faithful is perfectly explained by this phrase. The Church's work is to make saints of all of us, and to unite us in sanctity and through the sacraments and the proclamation of God's word to the body of Christ. Obedience always has this end in view: it is a discipline of mind and heart for the sake of the work of the Church.

Benedict's own experience of Nazism had taught him of the stupidity and wickedness of blind obedience. We have, of course, been taught to mistrust the call for obedience and to see lurking in the claims of obedience the abuse of power. Is it possible that one to whom we are called and required to be obedient can abuse that requirement? Of course! For which the Church needs an effective doctrine of sin and teaching on the extirpation of vice, rather than a hermeneutic of suspicion and a phenomenology of power. Is it possible that the Church as an institution can abuse the power entrusted to it? As we shall see, in the opinion of Benedict the Church is only an institution in a very dependent sense.

As Prefect of the Congregation for the Doctrine of the Faith, Benedict was certainly one of the men closest to the previous pope, and not without justice was he thought under John Paul II to be the second only to him in the daily working of the Catholic Church. There is no doubt that, following John Paul II, Benedict gave shape and lent his formidable scholarly weight to the debates and issues that unfolded in the life of the previous papacy. The clarity and firmness of his voice did not please everyone. There is an irony here – it was sometimes said that there was no John Paul II without Joseph Ratzinger (as Prefect of the Congregation for the Doctrine of the Faith), no Cardinal Prefect without John Paul II. Now there is only Benedict, as Pope. We are likely to gain, therefore, a broader understanding of Joseph Ratzinger, and publicly to see sides of him not yet fully understood.

There is no doubt that John Paul II was the man for the period of his pontificate. No other pope could have presided over the bringing down of the Berlin Wall and the ending of the Communist tyrannies of Europe. No other pope could have held the Church together in a way that seemed at times a titanic singular act of will. His tireless travel and unceasing courage were a remarkable witness, especially in the events of his dying. Benedict is likely to build on and complete – in a way that is profoundly complementary to John Paul II's pontificate – the work he did, whilst setting a different, even quieter, tone, which will open up a new era for the Church.

One of the names most associated with criticism of Benedict in his time as Prefect is that of the Swiss theologian Hans Küng (1928–). Benedict and Küng became friends during the Second Vatican Council, and Küng was instrumental, if not decisive, in the process of Benedict joining the Faculty of Theology at

Tübingen, where Küng spent his entire teaching career. Küng was deprived of his *missio canonica* – the right to teach in a Catholic university or faculty of theology – in 1979, two years before Benedict became Prefect of the Congregation for the Doctrine of the Faith. Ejected from the Catholic faculty of theology, Küng carried on teaching at Tübingen in a chair specially created for him outside the Catholic and protestant faculties, until he retired. Although Benedict was consulted on the decision to deprive him of the right to teach at a Catholic faculty (as he was then one of the German bishops), he was only very tangentially involved in the decision. Küng, whose work had been under consideration and a matter of concern to the Congregation for the Doctrine of the Faith since 1967, has set the tone for the subsequent denunciations of 'Ratzinger the inquisitor'. Benedict, for his, part, has said almost nothing in reply.

It is almost impossible, in any juridical process, for those whose responsibility it is to give advice on particular situations at the same time to defend their own part in the process of advice, without materially affecting the cases concerned. It has always been possible for journalists to wheel out some outraged university professor or other, label him as 'a world class Catholic theologian', and then report his tears of fury at yet another example of 'the injustice of the Church's abuse of its authority and resistance to change'. In exchanges of these kinds the truth – which is often extremely complex and difficult, even for those directly involved – is rarely heard.

A figure with whom Benedict has clashed more directly is the German theologian Johannes Baptist Metz (1928–). In 1979, when Archbishop of Munich and Freising, Benedict blocked Metz's appointment to a chair in theology in Munich. Nevertheless, Metz noted in an article with the Munich-based newspaper *Süddeutsche Zeitung* that Benedict continued to seek a dialogue with him, writing in 1988 to ask if discussion between them could begin again. In 1998 dialogue did indeed resume, when Benedict was a main speaker at a symposium for Metz's seventieth birthday. Küng was loud in his attack on Metz for inviting

Benedict – suggesting that for Küng dialogue and discussion are less important than the need to take sides.

The Congregation for the Doctrine of the Faith is above all responsible for the teaching and practice of theology in the life of the Church. In practice the theologian's task is to discern a particular relationship to truth, one in which there is always a risk. The Congregation for the Doctrine of the Faith's own document on the vocation of the theologian (published in 1990) begins by arguing that 'theology has importance for the Church in every age' which means the theologian's work is 'also exposed to risks since it must strive to "abide" in the truth'. The theologian strives to take account of the new problems that confront the human spirit. The work of the Congregation for the Doctrine of the Faith is sometimes the 'sharp end' of that risk – the need on some occasions to call attention to possible dangers in the work of a few theologians. In the view of the Congregation (borne out in fact), it has intervened only very rarely and where it has believed intervention to be absolutely necessary.

Privately the Congregation for the Doctrine of the Faith itself stresses that its concerns are never personal. Benedict has noted that the main purpose of dispute and critique of theological work is that the simple faith of the Christian believer is what theology must serve, and which theologians must protect. More often than not the Congregation for the Doctrine of the Faith has struggled to accommodate those with whom it has disputed: if some, like Matthew Fox, have subsequently left the Catholic Church, eventually paths have been found for others, like Tissa Balasuriya, to reconcile them. Benedict is well aware of the immense pain involved in having ideas close to the heart put into question, especially at the official level. This is partly because of the experience of the near-collapse of his own *Habilitation*, partly because of his understanding of those like de Lubac and von Balthasar whom he admired and has been close to but who themselves were at times under suspicion. It is not wrong for theological ideas to be tested and put under scrutiny – indeed it can be a privilege. If there is a genuine issue in the truth to be decided, the path of decision can be hard and even painful. Above all, the discernment of truth and the teaching of it (as a theologian) affects not only one's own pathway in the faith and one's own salvation, but the salvation of others. To teach falsely can put the relation of others to the truth at risk. To impair the faith of others is to put your own salvation into question.

8

The Congregation for the Doctrine of the Faith: Two Questions

The Congregation for the Doctrine of the Faith is part of the Church's discernment of the relation of theology – and this really means the understanding of theologians, because what is at issue is a *living* tradition, a tradition that lives in the hearts and faith of the Church – to the questions of the age. This is not other than part of the Church's address to, and redemption of, the world in which she finds herself.

The affairs of individual theologians have been regularly – if not always well – documented in the press. To comment on them individually might seem to be making a judgement, which is outside my competence or proper concern. Two issues from Benedict's years as Prefect are, however, worthy of further discussion, as each in different ways illustrates both what his role has been in the Congregation, and how he has understood theology in relation to the life of the Church. Many other examples could have been chosen. One indicates the Church's refusal of a change, the other shows how a change in what the Church thinks can come about. Both are intimately connected with the Church's engagement with the modern world.

In 1968 a gathering under the umbrella of CELAM, an organization made up of the conferences of bishops of Latin America, came together at Medellín in Colombia to discuss the situation of the extreme poverty across the Latin American nations, coupled with the activities of the various military dictatorships that governed the nations represented. It was from here that the phrase 'the preferential option for the poor' originated. Three years later the theologian Gustavo Guttiérez (1928–) published his book *A Theology of Liberation*, which gave its name to a movement. Others quickly followed suit – Leonardo Boff, Juan Luís Segundo, José Porfirio Miranda to name but a few all published works. Much of their work – for instance, that of Miranda – relies on a rich and vigorous scriptural exegesis which shows the relation between the Church's prophetic call for justice for the poor and those on the social margins, and Scripture and the Tradition itself.

What was new about Liberation Theology was that in the emphasis on concern for the poor and condemnation of oppression there was a strong political thrust, often Marxist in character. Some protestant Latin American theologians took this analysis very far indeed – José Miguez Bonino, for instance, with his book *Doing Theology in a Revolutionary Situation*. Liberation Theology in fact had its roots not only in Latin America but also in the political theology of Metz and the work of the German protestant theologian Jürgen Moltmann (1926–), and many of the central figures in Liberation Theology (Boff, Guttiérez, Segundo, among others) had in fact been trained in European, especially German, universities, a fact which Benedict had discussed in an article in 1984.

In September 1984 the Congregation for the Doctrine of the Faith issued an 'Instruction on Certain Aspects of the Theology of Liberation' which clarified both what was positive and what was negative about much of what Liberation Theology argued, but more importantly, identified dangers in the directions in which it was headed. Central to these was the concern that the Church must not collapse into the world – which means that, as one commentator put it, 'Marxism must not be "baptized"'. The Church cannot endorse political ways of analysing the world – in particular, the Church cannot endorse the Marxist concept of the class struggle. Christianity preaches a salvation yet to come, *after* the end of time, and so not *within* time, even though it must be witnessed to here and now. Although the Church is a sign of the coming Kingdom of God, it is not yet – even in itself – the realization of that Kingdom, still less does the Church authorize any present political or utopian goals.

A major concern of the Congregation for the Doctrine of the Faith's, and indeed of Benedict's, was that Liberation Theology in its

sharpest form took orthodox Christian dogmas and reinterpreted them through a Marxist
lens. In its most extreme form the truth of
specific dogmas, and even of the sacraments
themselves, is reduced to 'praxis', to what is
done rather than to what the dogmas and the
sacraments are in themselves: the only goal is
the political effort to realize social justice.
Coupled with the critique of the over-emphasis
on praxis was a concern about the misplace-
ment of eschatology, of what we may hope for
in this world as opposed to what we are to
hope for in the world to come. Marxism has
consistently promised in revolutionary activity
the transformation of the present world.
Christian eschatology, understood like this,
becomes an instrument for changing the
world, not the means by which Christians, in
the course themselves of being transformed by
God, proclaim God's truth to a fallen world
and thereby make manifest the hope of
redemption.

In fact, since Leo XIII's Encyclical on justice
for the poor and the vices of industrialization, *Rerum Novarum* of 1891, the Church has

continued to make a sharp critique both of social injustice and of the need to assist the poor. Successive popes have renewed this teaching, up to John Paul II's Encyclical *Centesimus Annus*, issued in 1991 on the hundredth anniversary of *Rerum Novarum*.

Two things should be stressed: the first is that a continued dialogue was kept up between both John Paul II and (during his time as Prefect) Benedict, with the bishops of Latin America and the Latin American situation. This dialogue had even begun for Benedict under Pope John Paul I (1978) who had sent Benedict as his representative to Latin America shortly after being elected pope in 1978. Although there is still scalding poverty, the political situation of Latin America is already much transformed (the dictatorships have largely disappeared), although this transformation is uneven, and there is much further to go. At the same time, perhaps less well heard, Benedict has in the past spoken of the evils of 'Americanism' – of the unbridled activity of globalization and a capitalism unfettered by social responsibility. The second is that a

concern of the document in 1984, and the subsequent discussions and visits of John Paul II
to Latin America, was to bring the work of the
Liberation Theologians back into a proper
focus – to criticize certain tendencies in Liberation Theology, but not all that was said or
written. Indeed, Liberation Theology has only
been *one* response to the Latin American situation. Benedict himself noted that 'for the very
poor, the prospect of a better world that
Liberation Theology held out to them was too
far away'. He has pointed out that the reception of Liberation Theology has itself been
uneven, with the effect in some areas of driving away the very ones it seeks to address.

In one other matter during Benedict's
Prefecture the Congregation for the Doctrine
of the Faith acted not to condemn, but to
undo a condemnation that was at best amb-
iguous, at worst unjust. In his 1998 Encyclical
Letter *Fides et Ratio*, John Paul II effectively
rehabilitated a figure from the nineteenth
century, almost in passing, by connecting
his work with positive understanding of the
relationship between faith and philosophy.

Fr. Antonio Rosmini (1797–1855), founder of the religious order the 'Institute of Charity' or Rosminians (not dissimilar in their constitution to the Jesuits), was also a prolific writer, whose voluminous works are still to this day being translated into English. Rosmini had been one of the consulters appointed by Pope Pius IX to consider the dogma of the Immaculate Conception prior to its being promulgated in 1854.

In 1849 two of Rosmini's books were placed on the 'Index', the list of prohibited books which was maintained up until 1948 (with a final demise in 1966), until in 1854 (the year before Rosmini's death) the then Congregation of the Index decreed that they could be taken off, because investigation had found nothing disparaging against the author. In 1887, however, a further investigation, this time by the precursor of the Congregation for the Doctrine of the Faith, the Holy Office, listed forty propositions taken from Rosmini's works that were condemned. In 2001 Benedict, as Prefect of the Congregation for the Doctrine of the Faith, issued a 'Note on the

1. *Above*: Pupil Joseph Ratzinger with his knapsack in Aschau am Inn, Germany, at end of 1932

2. *Below*: Family picture of father Joseph (right) and mother Maria (centre) Ratzinger with their children Maria, Georg and Joseph jr. (left–right) taken after both sons became priests in the Roman Catholic church

3. Joseph Ratzinger (right) and his brother Georg
wait together with 42 other men for their ordination
to the priesthood in Munich, Germany, 29 June 1951

4. Then German Cardinal Joseph Ratzinger
in Vatican City, 1978

5. Pope John Paul II (left) during a meeting with
then Cardinal Joseph Ratzinger in Munich,
Germany, November 1980

6. The Cardinal Joseph Ratzinger (centre) blessing the faithful during a religious procession before the consecration of Radom's new bishop Zygmunt Zimowski in May 2002

7. Then Cardinal Joseph Ratzinger (left) and former
Italian president Francesco Cossiga (right) during their
visit to the institute Maggiore di Bressanone,
near Bolzano in August 2004

8. *Above*: Newly elected Pope Benedict XVI stands
on the balcony of St. Peter's Basilica,
Vatican City, Tuesday 19 April 2005

9. *Below*: Cardinals pose with newly elected Pope
Benedict XVI for a group photo at the Vatican, Wednesday,
20 April, 2005. Benedict, the former Cardinal Joseph
Ratzinger of Germany, listed top priorities of his
pontificate in a lengthy message read in Latin to cardinals
gathered for the first Mass celebrated by the 265th leader
of the Roman Catholic Church

10. Pope Benedict XVI, flanked by Cardinal Camerlengo
Edoardo Martinez Somalo of Spain (left) and
Cardinal Angelo Sodano of Italy, signs a document
in his new studio at the Vatican

Force of the Doctrinal Decrees Concerning
the Thought and Work of Fr. Antonio Rosmini
Serbati'. Effectively the Note removes the suggestion of censure from the 1887 investigation.

Two reasons are given in the 'Note' for the
change: first, that the climate in which theology
was done at the time, the 'Thomism', especially,
that represented the way the work of St.
Thomas Aquinas was interpreted at the time,
prevented a proper reading of Rosmini's works.
The second factor was that 'the condemned propositions were mostly extracted from posthu-
mous works of the author. These works were
published without a critical apparatus capable
of defining the precise meaning of the expres-
sions and concepts used. This favoured a het-
erodox interpretation of Rosminian thought'.

The note recognizes that the real driving
force of Rosmini's work was that 'he was trying
to offer new possibilities to Catholic doctrine
in the face of the challenges of modern
thought'. Here again is a central concern of
Benedict's, which he recognizes in the work of
another theologian: the relation of the Church

to the world in which it finds itself and which it is to proclaim the redemption offered by Christ the Lord. The 'Note' remarks that this attempt to address the contemporary situation was on the one hand characterized by 'great courage and daring', even 'a certain rashness' but that the spiritual impulse under which Rosmini worked was honoured 'even by his staunch enemies'.

It could be said that vindication of this kind is worth little after a theologian is dead, until we recall that even the condemnation of the forty propositions only took place after Rosmini had died. The effects of a theologian's work can long outlive him – and here is the risk and the requirement for courage, both at the time and long after.

9

Benedict and the Press

In English there are already two biographical books concerning Pope Benedict XVI. The first is by Benedict himself. These are memoirs written in 1997 and covering the first fifty years of his life up to the point where he was made bishop of the ancient diocese of Munich and Freising in 1977. Published in English as *Milestones*, these memoirs are much to be commended to anyone who wants to gain more than the fleeting glimpse I have room to give of Benedict's life. The second, published in 1998 (a year after the first), is by John Allen, a reporter for perhaps the most influential Catholic newspaper in America, the *National Catholic Reporter*. Entitled *Cardinal Ratzinger: The Vatican's Enforcer of the Faith*, it is an attempt to explain not just the man, but also his role before he became pope, of Cardinal

Prefect of the Congregation for the Doctrine of the Faith.

At times it has been difficult – if not impossible – to see the distinction between the man and the office: between what the man Joseph Ratzinger thought and held personally, and what the Cardinal Prefect was required to publish in the name of the Church. In this there is something of the humility and simplicity of Benedict: as Cardinal Prefect it was less important that people understood the man than the office – and to think in this way is both his genuine attitude of service to the needs of the Church and a sense of sacrifice. That distinction between man and office has been further complicated by the way in which the public face of the Church, and especially the Vatican, has been shaped by the organs of mass communication. No public institution escapes the way that newspapers, television and radio all shape and manage public debate. The 'media' both help us to see, and often at the same time obscure, our access to what is going on behind the scenes, behind the rippling curtains of every public balcony, not just the Church's. Politics in the West – in Britain and North America especially – has itself taken on a form utterly intertwined with the way journalism functions. Journalists have two problems: first, how to make complex matters digestible to a public whom they presume is only partially well-informed; inevitably journalism flattens and forces into oppositions discussions and debates which are highly complex and nuanced when properly understood. Too often, however, both journalists and we who consume their work forget that this is what they do. Journalism all too frequently ends up spreading falsehood in the name of making the truth available to all. The second problem journalists have is as pernicious for truth as the first. The proliferation of newspapers, magazines, television and radio channels means there is simply a vast amount of media capacity to be filled. Hitherto, events drove the news; now, the news quite often drives events. Events themselves – this is especially true of politics – are now deliberately shaped to be digestible and intelligible to the industry of mass communication.

Britain and America suffer in this respect most of all. In Germany and France, for instance, as in all other European nations, there is a long tradition of 'high-brow' journalism available to a relatively wide audience. An example of this is the 'Feuilleton' section in each of two renowned German papers, the *Frankfurter Allgemeine Zeitung* and the intellectual weekly *Die Zeit*, which reports matters at a depth rarely attained in British journalism, possibly with the exception of the weekly *Economist* (and the Feuilleton section of both these German papers has taken a particular interest in Benedict, before and after his election to the papacy). In the countries of the former Soviet bloc, the cost of attaining a free press is an all too recent memory, and jealously guarded. News, however disseminated, is here rightly treated both with a not-unhealthy scepticism, whilst at the same time providing not just sound-bite reportage but also discerning commentary. The Church has rightly disdained being driven by the concerns and methods of the media, and yet has not entirely been able to remain free from the effects of their methods. Above all differences in the Church, often arcane and difficult even for experts to see for themselves, let alone for these experts to give to others good account of in their contours and shape, have been reduced in the press to supposed squabbles between 'conservatives', 'radicals' or 'reformers' driven by personalities, or the supposed drive for 'power', the ubiquitous root of the hermeneutic of suspicion that the post-war period has taught us all to bring to bear when viewing the activities of institutions.

Real questions in the life of the Church, as in the life of all human institutions and in human lives themselves, can take at longest centuries, at times decades, certainly years to unfold. Often when we think we are being denied the truth by the power-plays of others, what we are in fact denied is the ability to discern it well for ourselves. More often yet we have been tempted to throw aside a proper reserve – and wait for the issues to become clear – because we think we are owed (or we are being pressed to give) answers to questions we do not yet fully understand or see. In

Benedict a man has been elected whose own life and writings can be understood as a work of discernment of the post-war Church. Understood like this it will perhaps become clearer why he has been so decisive a choice.

Already the peculiar weakness of the Anglophone press was visible in the endless discussions in the media about the outcome of the conclave. The press presented the options and the possible candidates for pope (the cardinals who were *'papabile'*) exactly as they would in a political election, discussing blocks and factions, what this or that group wanted in this or that candidate and what each *papabile* cardinal's relative support was likely to be among the electors. It has sometimes been said that Christianity 'invented' the tradition of democracy in the West by the example of the way, according to the *Rule* of St. Benedict, an abbot is elected in a monastery. There is a silliness in this view: the home of democracy is the Athens of ancient Greece (and not all ancient Greece was democratic, by any means, nor even Athens in all its ancient history), not a monastic election; but there also is something to be learned from St. Benedict in this matter. In his *Rule*, St. Benedict reminds the monks that their task in electing an abbot is not to choose whom *they* would want, but to discern the mind of Christ himself for the future of the monastery. St. Benedict speaks of the need for a man of meritorious life and wise teaching, who will strive more to be loved than feared.

Walking across a Catholic university campus in the United States the day after the conclave began, I found (perhaps because I was in clerical dress) a microphone and camera thrust at me with the question 'what do you think about the fact that the conclave is deadlocked?' In previous centuries conclaves have taken sometimes years, not hours to choose the next pope: serious thought of deadlock might only have arisen in the modern era after a month or so. I suggested they come back in three years, if no pope had emerged (the length of time it took to choose Pope Gregory X [1271–1276]) – then we could talk about deadlock. As I evaded the interviewer's questions ('who do you want to be pope?'; 'what is the biggest issue facing the Church?') I could not have known that at that very moment Benedict had in fact been elected, and the cardinals were singing the ancient hymn of thanksgiving that is always sung on joyous moments in the Church's life – the *Te Deum laudamus* – in the Sistine Chapel: 'we praise *you*, O God'. The brevity of the conclave revealed all talk of factions and parties to be irrelevant, and the pace of the event itself brushed all this aside. The work of the conclave is not so much a political act, the election of a man to high office, but rather the difficult and precarious task of discerning the mind of God for his Church.

No less affected by the journalistic weaknesses of the English-speaking nations is John Allen's biography of the Pope, for if it is well-researched and carefully – even respectfully – written, it betrays a peculiarly American and English-speaking perplexity about its subject, a perplexity that this book has already commented on in the difficulty of Americans especially, but also most contemporary Europeans, to remember or understand the grim political situation of Germany even before 1933. This is not just my opinion of Allen's book – it was confirmed by Allen himself when he said, just a week after the Pope's election 'if I were to write the book again today, I'm sure it would be more balanced, better informed, and less prone to veer off into judgment'. Allen speaks of how he came to understand his own book entirely differently because of a review written by someone he knew and respected, a Fr. Joseph Komonchak. Let me quote at length what John Allen said in his own paper (the *National Catholic Reporter*) about this review, because it will help introduce a question central to the present book. Allen says:

It was not, let me be candid, a positive review. Fr. Komonchak pointed out a number of shortcomings and a few errors, but the line that truly stung came when he accused me of 'Manichean journalism'. He meant that I was locked in a dualistic mentality in which Ratzinger was consistently wrong and his critics consistently right. I was initially crushed, then furious. I re-read the book with Fr. Komonchak's criticism in mind, however, and reached the sobering conclusion that he was correct. The book – which I modestly believe is not without its merits – is nevertheless too often written in a 'good guys and bad guys' style that vilifies the cardinal. It took Fr. Komonchak pointing this out, publicly and bluntly, for me to ask myself, 'Is this the kind of journalist I want to be?' My answer was no, and I hope that in the years since I have come to appreciate more of those shades of gray that Fr. Komonchak rightly insists are always part of the story.

Allen has had to confront the embarrassing discovery that in attempting to tell the mere facts, judiciously and well, he failed to tell the truth – or rather he told only part of the truth. He failed to take into account who *he* was, and what he took for granted as self-evidently obvious to him (but not necessarily to those who see it differently), in narrating the life of Joseph Ratzinger. He ended up, in his own words, by vilifying his subject because of his own short-sightedness. In this we should have considerable sympathy for John Allen, for he is not different from all of us who have been taught to believe that if we just marshall the 'facts' the truth will shine out from them self-evidently, so that we can make a clear judgement and come to a conclusion that *everyone* would reach who knew what we knew. This has been the optimistic myth of the outlook of especially the nineteenth and twentieth centuries, that truth is reducible to a certain kind of mere rationalism.

It is never as simple as this. The way in which the facts are brought together, the way in which they are told, will itself determine what they say. In a court of law, deliberating what happened in a sequence of events is always a precarious affair. No two witnesses ever see quite the same thing in the same way – what they see is often coloured by their relation to the defendant or the matter or events in question: hidden factors emerge and can become decisive for the outcome of the trial which were not visible at the beginning.

This is not the same as saying that (in our example of a trial) there was not an actual or real event – or that what each person sees is true 'for him'. This is the 'dictatorship of relativism' that Benedict mentioned in his homily to the cardinals as their Dean, immediately prior to the conclave which elected him. This relativism is what Benedict has so often decried as corroding the very heart of life itself, especially in Europe (but nowhere else is immune from this corrosion). Rather when there is a matter of truth to be understood, there really is something at issue, something *there* to be known – but we must become aware of the manner of our approach, of how we are enquiring into the issue. What we know of what is 'there' is shaped by our different manners of approach, and the different ways in which our eyes have been trained to see when they look out. A discipline and generosity, a familiarity with the ways of truth, are required to discern truth well – not just a totting up of 'the facts'.

Allen begins his book by painting a picture of two churches – one he describes as a 'post-Vatican II' Church. This Church is full of people who are liberal-minded, socially concerned, who have grown accustomed to change in the interior life of the Church. He gives the example of hearing his pastor one Sunday describe the new rites of confession when they were introduced in the 1970s, and asking himself 'what would change next?' He 'took for granted that church practices and structures were fluid, that they could evolve'. He describes this kind of Catholicism as faithful, but evolving, open to dissent, engaged with society, and calls it 'mainstream'. Allen is therefore perplexed and bewildered by the constant discovery that for Benedict, the structures of the Church are not fluid and do not evolve, that dissent means something quite different for Benedict than for him, and that Benedict's engagement with society – which we shall see, is a decisive concern for him – takes a very different form to the one with which Allen is familiar. The other Church that emerges from Allen's view is, therefore, rigid and conservative, inflexible and outdated.

If Allen describes his understanding of the Church as 'mainstream' one would have to reply that except within its own terms, it is anything but. It is, at most, a few decades old, and narrowly focused on North America and Western Europe, compared to an ethos which is mainstream in the sense of being centuries-old and which manifested itself in a recognizably familiar way everywhere in the world it was carried.

The habits of mind that we have cultivated, and our predispositions to see some things in one way and not another will be decisive in all matters of truth. A cabinet-maker will view a chest of drawers with regard to the quality of the wood and the craftsmanship; a dealer with regard to who he knows that will be attracted to a particular style; a connoisseur will know how the chest compares to others of its age or type, and the history into which it fits, by nationality and region perhaps, or by period. Someone with no expertise, no discipline or training, no sense of this chest or its provenance will be reduced to saying 'I like it' or 'I don't like it'. In matters of chests this is not terribly important, but when the majority of our judgements take this form, over matters of real import for our daily lives, and when we have convinced ourselves that we are saying something decisive and material in our 'I like it' or 'I don't like it', then these are the truly relativistic judgements that corrode life. Judgements like this are not formed on the basis of anything beyond the self, they just express a momentary opinion – they are truly empty, even when they seem to have content or be concerned with the truth.

THREE

Aspects of the Thought

10

The Theologian of Vatican II

Benedict XVI has said of the Second Vatican Council that it is a Council whose time is yet to come. Could it be that he is the Pope to usher in this Council's moment? It is well known (as we shall see) that he was indirectly an influence on the Council, and that already by the end of it, even as a young theologian, he had worries both about some of its statements and about how the Council was being understood and implemented. It is true that a certain enthusiasm for the Council overtook the Church, and changed it beyond all recognition. It is also true that in its wake many have rejected, and more have questioned, that period of enthusiasm and its consequences. Some – self-styled 'conservatives' of an extreme kind, – have even equated the enthusiasm of the post-conciliar era with the need to reject the

Council itself. Benedict is often called a conservative – and so placed among those who might at least have sharp questions about the Council and its consequences. And yet his approach – that this Council's time is yet to come – is not conservative, but radical, a return to the very roots of what enthused those who watched and even participated in the Council's unfolding. Above all Benedict was in touch with the men who articulated the ferment of ideas that gave rise to the Council's discussions and statements, and with the currents of ideas that swirled around the Council; men whom he had been reading while a doctoral and *Habilitation* student, almost all of whom he at one time or another met and had friendly relations with – the Jesuits Karl Rahner (1904–1984) and Henri de Lubac, Hans Urs von Balthasar, the Dominican Yves Congar (1904–1995), but also the proponents of the liturgical movement – the German theologian Romano Guardini (1885–1968), and the Benedictine Odo Casel (1886–1948).

We will come to look more closely at Benedict's concerns for the Church's Sacred

Liturgy, but one aspect of all of this is instructive. One of the ways in which Benedict has been understood is as a young reformer who, as he grew older, turned conservative in distaste at the developments in the Church during and after the Council. The example given is often of Benedict's early enthusiasm for the Liturgical Movement, and especially for the ideas of Guardini. It is certainly true that Guardini was hugely influential in Germany at precisely the time when Benedict was growing up, and Benedict speaks warmly in his memoirs of both his love for the liturgy and the fact that even the parish of his boyhood in Traunstein was not untouched by the Liturgical Movement.

In pursuit of a deeper involvement and understanding of the laity at celebrations of the Mass Guardini had certainly pursued an approach that was (for his day) experimental. Guardini had shared in the discussions and events at the Monastery of Maria Laach in the Rhineland, a centre of interest in liturgical reform which, almost from the beginning of the twentieth century, had been at the heart of the Liturgical Movement. He had celebrated Mass facing toward the people (always at least a theoretical possibility even before Vatican II), and long before it was fully licit had experimented with the use of the vernacular for some of the people's parts of the Mass. He had encouraged a form of the Mass that later become known as the 'dialogue Mass', where not only those in the sanctuary but also the people in the congregation made some or even all of the responses to the priest. Benedict's early and vigorous interest in Guardini has been interpreted as evidence of his reforming approach, an approach that he is said later to have abandoned.

Important then, is Benedict's own understanding of Guardini. Benedict has argued that 'Guardini split off from Maria Laach' because the theologians and liturgists gathered there 'had taken up a purist position'. In fact what drew Benedict – even before the Council – to Guardini was his historical sensitivity and his undogmatic respect for the real heart of all questions in liturgical reform: that the ordinary layman should better understand, share in, and love the mystery that the Liturgy (especially the Mass) is. More recently he has written against the 'fanaticisms that have not been uncommon in the controversies of the last forty years' which have precluded 'carefully listening to each other'. In this context he has added 'the labelling of positions as "preconciliar", "reactionary", and "conservative" or as "progressive" and "alien to the faith" achieves nothing: what is needed is a new mutual openness'. To understand Benedict's attitude to the Second Vatican Council it is necessary, therefore, not to look at what we think was happening to *him* psychologically, but to look at the Council as he himself looks at it.

Benedict's first chair of theology, in Bonn in 1959, coincided with the beginning of a friendship that was to propel him to the centre-stage of the debates around the Second Vatican Council. The visible changes in the Catholic Church in the last forty years have been more dramatic and far-reaching than the changes of the last four hundred. No aspect of Catholic life has been left untouched by what appeared to be unleashed by the Second Vatican Council.

Announced by Pope John XXIII in 1959, less than three months after he was elected, the Council met in four autumn sessions in St. Peter's Basilica between 1962 and 1965. In the formal sessions of the Council only the bishops and major superiors of religious orders could speak, in Latin. Around the formal Council sessions, and throughout the year, numerous special commissions reviewed and prepared the work of the Council, a work that resulted in no less than seventy-three documents of various kinds. John XXIII urged the Council 'to use the medicine of mercy rather than the weapons of severity' in their deliberations. John XXIII did not live to see even the second session of the Council, which was opened by his successor, Paul VI.

There is no doubt that the most influential voices in the Council were those of the German and French cardinals; it was in these countries, together as well as with the theologians in Flanders around the Dominican Edward Schillebeeckx (1914–), had developed the ideas the that drove the Council's discussions. Among the most important of these

French and German cardinals was Josef Frings (1887–1978), Archbishop of Bonn. Frings gave one of the most dramatic speeches of the Council, in the second session, when he publicly denounced the work of the Holy Office (later to become the Congregation for the Doctrine of the Faith), and by implication its Pro-Prefect, Alfredo Cardinal Ottaviani. One of Frings' closest advisers throughout the Council was a young German theologian, recently appointed to a chair in theology in his diocese: the future Benedict XVI. Frings had appointed Benedict his *peritus*, that is, his formal adviser at the Council.

Here again we must exercise caution in understanding the relation between the young theologian and the cardinal. Too much has been made of the identity between what Frings said and what Benedict must – it is supposed – have therefore told him to say. First, no theologian, however able, is likely to turn a cardinal into his mouthpiece (and Frings was very much his own man); second, there is much evidence, if we read Benedict's own words carefully, to suggest – as much with Frings as later with John Paul II – that Benedict has always taken the role of adviser with great seriousness. Those who receive advice do not always follow it; the specific advice required may not necessarily correspond to the adviser's own mind.

Nevertheless, Benedict was active in presenting ideas and providing vigorous advice not only to Frings, and not only alone, but to many of the cardinals, and often together with other theologians. Benedict was crucial in shaping the final version of the text that eventually became the 1964 Dogmatic Constitution on the Church, *Lumen Gentium*. He was intimately involved in the discussions that took place behind the Council's deliberations, and in profound dialogue with those not less influential than himself.

11

Vatican II and What Followed

Benedict has said that Vatican II is upheld by the same authority as Vatican I (1869–1870) and the Council of Trent (1545–1563). He has added that, for a Catholic, 'it is impossible to take a position *for* or *against* Trent or Vatican I' and in the same way it is impossible to decide for or against Vatican II. In many of his writings Benedict has stressed the continuity between the pre- and post-conciliar Church that many have either overlooked or even sought to deny. One of the Pope's major concerns has been how the Council began to be seen 'like a great church parliament, that could change and reshape everything according to its own desires'. He notes that a question arose – above all in the hearts of ordinary lay people and of many priests – 'If the bishops in Rome could change the faith (as it appeared they could), why only the bishops?' He has observed that many of the 'concrete effects' of Vatican II – the Church as it is today – 'do not correspond to the intentions of the Council Fathers'. Therefore he has called for a 'return to the authentic texts of the original Vatican II'. Benedict first began to raise his concerns with the ways in which the Council was being interpreted as early as 1966, first in a lecture given at Münster and then in one at Bamberg.

Benedict does not believe that either the fundamental truth of the faith *could* have been changed by the Council, or that indeed it *was* changed. It is in this sense that the Council is yet fully to be understood or have its day. A key phrase, enigmatically inserted into the first statement to be approved by the Council, might explain this well. In the Dogmatic Constitution on the Liturgy, *Sacrosanctum Concilium* (1963), at the very beginning, there is a sentence that speaks of the need 'better accommodate to the necessities of our times those structures which are subject to change'. At first reading a phrase like this suggests that there are many things in the Church which can be changed, and that the basis for changin them arises from the nature of the times we live in. This comes very close to the mentality which Benedict has spoken of which afflicts the contemporary Church and more widely modern humanity, especially in the West. His words on modern, affluent, man (whether a believer or not) have been harsh – he speaks of 'a tertiary bourgeoisie' – a wealthy élite who are characterized by, and foment, a 'liberal-radical ideology of individualistic, rationalistic and hedonistic stamp'. Elsewhere he has spoken of the way in which modern man is consumed by the view that everything is manipulable for himself as if everything were merely instruments or tools in his hands.

Benedict has spoken of two complementary forces at work: first, the 'unleashing *within* the Church of latent polemical and centrifugal forces; and *outside* the Church ... a cultural revolution in the West'. Above all Benedict has identified in the mentality that gripped the reception of the Council the belief that from now on all theological discussion was predominantly in the hands of scholars and experts. Coupled with this are his often over-looked remarks on his disappointment with the discussion in the Council's sessions on the place of the laity. It was not that the laity were given the wrong prominence – either too much or too little – but that there was a widespread misunderstanding of the place of the laity in the unfolding of the drama of salvation. Benedict has spoken of how, coupled with this misunderstanding, there was an overemphasis on the idea, new to the Council, of the 'People of God' which gave birth to a conception of a 'Church from below' or a 'Church of the People'. This, he said, became the 'goal of reform'.

Where Benedict did become concerned about the actual debate in the Council was over the Pastoral Constitution on the Church in the Modern World – *Gaudium et Spes*. It is sometimes said that this is where the essential agreement between the French and German theologians broke down – where the French view, especially some of the ideas of the French Jesuit Teilhard de Chardin (1881–1955) 'tri-umphed'. De Chardin developed a remarkably speculative theology of man's endless evolution to a higher state, through being infused with the divinity of God. In this sense man is ever-evolving to a more divine state.

In Benedict's view *Gaudium et Spes* underplayed the importance of a doctrine of sin. We must recall that a doctrine of sin is not, from a Christian point of view, a doctrine of denunciation and punishment. It is above all through an adequate theology that explains the place of sin and our own situation as sinners that we encounter the necessity and gift of salvation itself. In the great proclamation of the Easter liturgy, the *Exsultet* chant that begins the vigil liturgy after the Easter fire has been blessed, the deacon sings of the *felix culpa*, the 'blessed fault' and necessary sin of Adam that ushers in the incarnation, death and resurrection of Christ. It is in discovering ourselves to be sinners that we discover our need of God. It is here, therefore, that Benedict questioned what he saw as the impaired emphasis in *Gaudium et Spes* of both the doctrine of sin and the doctrine of salvation in its relation to contemporary man.

If modern man is to be addressed by the Church (as he is in *Gaudium et Spes*) with such optimism then, Benedict asked, 'what is salvation all about? What does its totality mean for man, if he can be described perfectly well without it?' It is not so much that *Gaudium et Spes* is wrong or in error, as that the correct emphasis is obscured by a misplaced optimism. *True* optimism is in the redemption promised through Jesus Christ, where man and all of fallen creation can be renewed through God's saving action, made manifest in his Son. Here then we can see a different, indeed more adequate, interpretation that should belong to the phrase that urges better accommodation to 'the needs of the times'. For a better accommodation would find the right way to address modern man with his sinfulness and need of salvation. This does not mean that the Church has to be adapted to modern man's critical suggestions for a Church in which he might feel more accommodated and at home *as an unredeemed person*, but rather that man's own tendency toward regarding everything as subject to change and manipulation for the sake of his own immediate desires occasions him to lose sight of his sinfulness. What is needed here is a *way in* for modern man to understand and desire his need of salvation, not an accommodation to the immaturity and imperfection of his unredeemed situation.

Accommodation to the needs of the times – like John XXIII's own exhortation to apply the medicine of mercy – is a call for the Church to engage with the modern world with a pastoral heart – advised, but not dictated to, by its experts and scholars. This means that it is not the deposit of faith that has changed, nor even that the way in which the deposit is to be presented is changed, but rather that strenuous means are to be sought to make the deposit of faith available to the contemporary situation.

Those who have styled themselves as conservatives have perhaps better understood this than those – calling themselves liberal, or being so called by their 'conservative' detractors – who have sought (or appeared to seek) to 'change' the deposit of faith in order to make it more palatable to modern humanity.

Where the so-called 'conservatives' have fallen down most, perhaps, is in styling themselves as standing in opposition to all that the world is and stands for. To turn the Church into a refuge for the pure is as inimical to its pastoral mission as to empty out its treasure-house in the name of modernization and relevance. For Christians are as much formed by, and are a product of, the world in which we live as anybody else. Benedict points out – specifically in emphasizing the continuity of the teaching of Vatican II with what preceded it – that 'it is not Christians who oppose the world, but rather the world which opposes itself to them when the truth about God, about Christ and about man is proclaimed. The world waxes indignant when sin and grace are called by their names'. Thus it is not for Christians to set their faces against the world and denounce it, but rather to proclaim – with the courage of a refusal to conform or to be intimidated by the world – the redemption wrought in Christ.

12

Sacred Liturgy

Pope Benedict has written that 'the inex-
haustible reality of the Catholic liturgy has
accompanied me through all phases of life,
and so I shall have to speak of it again and
again'. Central to understanding Holy Saturday, the day between Good Friday and
Easter Day (the day on which Benedict was
born) is the anxious but joyful anticipation
with which the Church waits to meet her risen
Lord. All prayer is grounded in this mood of
anticipation – but at the same time all prayer
takes its root at the foot of the Cross of Christ.
Benedict has again and again emphasized that
the mystery of Christian worship is rooted
not in the communal self-expression of a worshipping community, but in the sacrifice of
Christ, and so in knowing that the price of our
redemption is the blood spilled for us by the

Son of God. Before the Cross, and in anticipation of the glorious resurrection of Christ and in our own expectation of resurrection, we can do nothing but wait in hope – and yet, on the contrary, everything is done for us by God.

In October 2004, shortly before he died, John Paul II declared the year until October 2005 a 'year of the Eucharist', in which the Church was, in part, called upon to meditate on the character and nature of the Sacred Liturgy. Even without this, it would seem that the liturgy of the Catholic Church will be an important focus of Benedict's papacy. How and why this should be so is profoundly connected with Benedict's understanding of theology, of Scripture and of revelation, which form a trilogy of chapters in this book.

In no other part of the Church's life have the changes since the Second Vatican Council been more visible than in her public worship, the Sacred Liturgy. In truth, these changes were under way even before the Council, although they were tightly controlled and their effects were less visible, especially outside France and Germany. France and Germany were the focus for, and in the driving seat of, liturgical change, in the form of the 'Liturgical Movement', which began as early as the beginning of the twentieth century (if not before with the writings of Abbot Guéranger [1805–1875]), and which we have observed Benedict was, especially as a younger man, keenly involved in. Pius X had already begun to make remarkable changes in Catholic life, by introducing frequent communion as a feature of Catholic worship, albeit not as frequent as now. In addition he opened up the reception of the Blessed Sacrament to children as soon as they attained the age of reason (seven years of age). As well, Pius X in 1911 reformed the Breviary – the daily prayer of the Church required to be said by all clergy and members of religious orders. Whereas in the Breviary before 1911 all one hundred and fifty of the psalms would have been said by every cleric and religious each week, now the psalms were distributed over something like a two-week period.

This reform points to an important feature of the Church's liturgy – that a very great deal of it is, and always has been, comprised of

Scripture. In addition to the rich and beautiful cursus of the psalms, the texts of the liturgy are made up from sections and readings from the Gospels, the other writings of the New Testament and the Old Testament. Those parts of the liturgy which are not directly taken from Scripture – the prayers especially, but even the ancient hymns and chants in use almost everywhere until very recently (and still available for use even today) – are rich in references to Scripture and are in everything they say, consonant with the way the Church has interpreted Scripture. In many ways the Sacred Liturgy *is* the 'official' or formal interpretation of Scripture employed by the Church (this is what the Tradition is).

The greatest changes in the Church's liturgy or practices of prayer have been perhaps that the liturgy is nowadays almost always in the vernacular – the ordinary language of the country where the liturgy is being celebrated. It will perhaps have come as a surprise to many to hear John Paul II's funeral liturgy, and Benedict XVI's inaugural Mass, take place in Latin. Latin has been the official liturgical

language of the Western Church since about
the second half of the fourth century and –
surprising to many – it still is. Many Catholics,
especially in the United States, believe (wrongly)
that special permission has to be got for Mass
to take place in Latin. In fact any Mass that is
not specifically designated to be in the vernacular *may* be said in Latin. Permission does
have to be obtained for the Mass to be said
in the form it took before the new missal
authorized by Paul VI in 1970, the so-called
'Tridentine rite'.

Benedict has commented on the initial pro-
hibition, and subsequent permissions under
very particular circumstances, of any use of
the form of Mass prior to 1970, when the new
Missale Romanum of Paul VI was introduced.
If the new missal brought with it 'a real
improvement and enrichment' the prohibi-
tion of the use of the earlier form 'makes the
liturgy appear to be no longer a living development, but the product of erudite work and
juridical authority'. He has said that, notwith-
standing certain pastoral problems, this
impression has caused tremendous harm,

because the view was formed that 'the liturgy is something "made", not something given in advance but lying within our own power of decision'. Benedict has repeatedly called for a way to be found to end the restrictions on the use of liturgical forms that existed prior to 1970, noting that those who are attached to them are sometimes 'treated like lepers. This intolerance is such that we have never seen anything like it in the whole history of the Church'. He has also noted that the Second Vatican Council did not itself reform the liturgy, but laid down conditions under which Mass should be celebrated. These conditions apply, Benedict has argued, irrespective of the rite used – they apply equally to the pre- and post-1970 rites.

The other major change in the Mass especially since 1970 is the atmosphere of informality that accompanies modern Catholic worship. In almost all Churches the priest now says Mass facing toward the congregation, where only a few years ago he would have done so facing East, and so most likely facing the same way as the congregation, at an altar

which would have seemed more remote and
distant than the arrangement current in many
churches. Benedict has stressed that even here
there are misunderstandings. Mass *may* be
said either facing East, or facing the people
(assuming these directions are different).
There is no prescription for either direction in
the laws of the Church for either the current
form of Mass or the form that predated 1970.
Benedict himself pointed out regarding the
disappearance of Latin and the direction of
the priest in the Mass, 'that neither is in fact
found in the decrees of the Council'. Benedict
has – taking up remarks of Fr. Louis Bouyer's
cong. orat. (1913–2004) made immediately
after the Council about the ubiquity of Mass
said facing the people – written in many places
about the merits of the celebration of Mass
where all (priest included) are facing East, or
emphasizing the question of the real 'direction' toward which priest and people alike
should face by placing a crucifix in a prominent place on the altar, so that all may understand themselves to be facing the sacrifice of
the Cross.

125

The Liturgical Movement had sought originally to understand the liturgy as – in
Benedict's words – 'a living network of tradition which had taken concrete form'. The pres-
sure for reform of the liturgy, even before the
Council, had the intention of opening up the
liturgy to greater understanding by the ordinary Catholic. The Pope clearly believes that
the reform that followed the Council went far
beyond what the Council itself expected.

Between 1968 and about 1978 a wholesale
revision of the various texts of the Catholic
liturgy was undertaken, leaving none untouched: with this revision went a wholesale
revision of the ways in which the liturgy is
done, with the virtual disappearance of the
ancient 'Gregorian' chant that had accompanied all its sung forms. The texts for the Mass,
or Missal, were revised from 1969 onward, from
top to bottom. The Breviary – the prayers for
the various parts of the day: the night or 'vigil'
office (matins), morning prayer (lauds), the
'hours' of the day – which once comprised
four, were reduced to three and shortened.
Evening prayer (vespers) was shortened, as

was Compline, the night prayer of the Church. The various rites of baptism, marriage, Christian death, confirmation, ordination and so on were all revised. The Ceremonial of Bishops was drastically simplified. The last of the liturgical books, the Martyrology, which comprises a record of the lives of the saints over the whole history of the Western Church and is set to be read in a section proper to each day of the year, was issued in 2001 in Latin and is yet to be translated. This revision has been so long in coming that the Martyrology has probably ceased to be used as part of the daily prayer of the Church except in just a very few places.

Benedict has spoken repeatedly of the way in which the changes in the liturgy, especially the Mass, were implemented, and of what in the changes was lost. In 1975, noting (against critics of Mass in the vernacular) that if on the one hand even Trent had foreseen the possibility of use of the language of the people, on the other there were concerns about the actual character of the liturgical reform, suggesting 'we shall have to examine the reforms already carried out'. His most strenuous concern, as we shall see later, is that 'however much the liturgy is simplified and rendered comprehensible, the mystery of God's action operating through the Church must remain untouched'. In 2000 he published a book, translated into English as *The Spirit of the Liturgy*, which traces the whole character and nature of the sacred activity of the Church and which draws attention to the importance of the *form* of the whole actions. He notes how the motor for many of the liturgical reforms was to foster a greater participation of all in the Sacred Liturgy. Pope Leo XIII had spoken of 'active participation' in the Mass, in a phrase that has almost become a watchword for liturgical reform. Benedict notes that 'the word was very quickly misunderstood to mean something external, entailing a need for general activity, as if as many people as possible, as often as possible, should be visibly engaged in action'. Benedict's reply to this misunderstanding is that 'the real "action" in the liturgy in which we are all supposed to participate is the action of God himself'. It is this that distinguishes all Christian worship from any other kind: 'God himself acts and does what is essential'.

In particular Benedict has been a vocal critic of what he sees as strong deficiencies in the ways in which much contemporary worship is undertaken. He has noted that the differences in the Liturgy 'as it is actually practised and celebrated in various places is often much greater than the difference between the old and new liturgies when celebrated according to the rubrics of the liturgical books', and that a particular danger for the Mass has been that a theology has increasingly arisen which under-plays the sacrificial character of the Mass and overemphasizes the aspect of it as an action of a particular worshipping community.

Benedict has been critical of the way in which the reform of the liturgy was under-taken, again stressing that 'to a great extent the specialists were listened to almost exclusively. A greater independence on the part of the pastors [bishops] would have been desirable'. He has at times called for a 'reform of the reform' of the liturgy, implying that a revision of the reform of the Mass would represent a return to the actual intentions of the Council Fathers at Vatican II. In this respect, he notes, 'the Council itself did not reform the liturgical books, but rather ordered their revision'. He has even spoken, not long before being elected, of the crisis of contemporary worship, and of how, having been moved by the desire to understand the liturgy in its historical richness at the time of the Council, he 'can only stand, deeply sorrowing, before the ruins' of the things the Liturgical Movement was concerned for. Elsewhere Benedict has said 'I am convinced that the crisis in the Church that we are experiencing today is to a large extent due to the disintegration of the Liturgy'. He has added 'for the Liturgy is not about us, but about God. Forgetting about God is the most imminent danger of our age'.

13

Sacred Scripture

Benedict has said of Sacred Scripture that 'exegesis has always remained for me the centre of my theological work'. No theologian adequate to his science can argue differently. Yet, as Benedict has been well aware, the place of Scripture in the life of the Church has been part of the 'crisis of the Church' of which he has spoken.

I have already written of the revision of the Church's Martyrology, the record of the lives of the Saints for use in the liturgy. The reasons for the revision of the Martyrology perhaps best explain the connection between the revision of the liturgical books and Scripture. The Martyrology is a compendium especially of histories of the earliest Christian Martyrs. Some of its contents were clearly the matter of legend, since by modern historical accounts the events described occasionally border on the fanciful. A great number of the stories of martyrdom it contains cannot be corroborated by any other evidence. The expressly stated intention of the revision was to bring it within the standards of modern historical accuracy – the same principles were employed for the revision of the Church's annual calendar, which in part governs her celebrations of the lives of the Saints. It is this drive for the 'historical' that has so traumatized both the Church's understanding of her own history – of which the Martyrs and Saints are a central part – and her understanding of Scripture.

Like the accounts of the martyrs, much of the Church's understanding of Scripture is in the traditions that she has held to be true but can nowhere corroborate. Benedict has noted that contemporary understandings of the historical have made the concept of tradition itself open to question, because modern historicism has no place for the oral tradition running alongside Scripture and – as he notes – reaching back to the apostles, 'hence offering another source of historical knowledge beside the Bible'. The Church's own history of interpretation *is* this tradition.

The large-scale changes in the Church's liturgical expression which I described in the last chapter have paralleled an entire transformation in Catholic theology of attitudes toward Scripture. These changes were already far advanced in the protestant faculties especially of Germany in the nineteenth century. Driven by the principles of the 'historical-critical method' and of various schools of 'criticism', the results have been, among many other things, the 'search for the historical Jesus'. This is the quest to unearth from 'beneath' the record of the books of the New Testament – especially the Gospels – the man Jesus and the events of his life, by separating him and these events from the layers of interpretation 'added' by the actual writers of the Gospels. Perhaps the strongest claims of the revolution in scriptural understanding – claims which are not at all new, but can be traced in their modern form back to the eighteenth century – concern the possibility that

Jesus could have understood himself to be the Son of God, or that there could have been a physical resurrection of Jesus, or that the historical man Jesus could actually have performed miracles of healing or feeding. Because these things are not seen today or cannot be repeated 'scientifically', the argument goes, they cannot be understood to be true in any meaningful sense.

The question of truth is once again paramount here. For the arguments for these kinds of biblical criticism – of dismantling the texts down to their actual historical reference – claim that the truth of Scripture is subordinate to what it is scientifically, philosophically or historically possible and so true. What this means is that instead of the measure of truth being witnessed to and made manifest in the Scriptures, now the Scriptures are subordinated to a purely 'scientific' understanding of what is or can be true. This raises a question to which Benedict has given a most important but little-understood answer – in what way does Scripture reveal what is true? Before we can reach this question, we must first examine a second, almost opposing tendency that the Pope has traced in his writing, one not less damaging to the Catholic faith.

For if on the one hand Scripture has been reduced only to what is written, not the tradition of interpretation that has always accompanied what was written, Benedict suggests that a mood gripped the Church after the Second Vatican Council to argue that Scripture was complete in matters of faith. This means that rather than Scripture being explained by the Church's tradition and amplified by it, on the contrary, there could be nothing in the Church's tradition or teaching that is not directly and simply justified by Scripture.

Two opposed movements come together here: on the one hand, as Benedict argues, only what is in Scripture can justify what the Church believes. On the other hand, the Scriptural writers can no longer be trusted because no single scriptural author can be trusted to have recorded matters as we ourselves might record them now, with the stringent standards of historical accuracy we would apply today. He suggests that the Church after the Council has largely been caught between these two poles of interpretation.

Here, all at once, can be seen the extreme relativism toward which every believer is now to be driven. What this amounts to, Benedict suggests, is that 'believing amounted to having opinions and was in need of constant revision'.

What Benedict identifies here are tendencies to a kind of historicism and textual empiricism. In the midst of these developments, there have, of course, been real insights and work of real importance. He suggests that 'the historico-critical interpretation has certainly opened many and momentous possibilities for a better understanding of the biblical text'. Benedict has argued that the dangers, however, of the contemporary understanding of Scripture are that only the exegetical expert may comment on the meaning of sacred texts – to the detriment even of the theologian who is not himself an exegete, let alone the ordinary believer.

If Benedict's understanding of the developments in the practice of exegesis and biblical study has, whilst understanding the positive aspects, also been acutely aware of the potentially negative effects, on what is his own understanding of Scripture based? Benedict's own theological outlook has been profoundly shaped by the Church Fathers and also by the Scholastic tradition. The writings of the Fathers are suffused with Scripture – there are passages of the *Sermons* of St. Bernard of Clairvaux, for just one example, which are almost entirely comprised of citations of the psalms. The Fathers, who gave loving shape to the *traditio* (not so much 'tradition' as – translated literally – what they believed was 'handed on' to them by the Apostles) understood Scripture in a richer and more complex way than many contemporary experts.

Benedict himself has spoken of how much contemporary exegesis is preoccupied with the historiographical past – the context in which the Scriptures (especially the books of the Old Testament) were written, parallels between these books and similarly writings in parallel contexts. To understand the origins of the Scriptures, these things are indeed important, although we should bear in mind that much of this study has to base itself on theories of interpretation, some of which are highly speculative. If, for instance, you believe it impossible for a person to be raised from the dead or be taken alive into heaven, this will without doubt colour your historical investigations into a text that speaks of God's gathering the prophet Elijah to himself, or the raising of Lazarus, or the resurrection of Jesus himself.

Among the foremost of the patristic exegetes is a theologian whom Benedict himself has studied in great depth (and whom we have already encountered) – St. Augustine of Hippo. Augustine speaks of Scripture both as a 'bottomless well' of meaning, and as having a past, a present and a future. Augustine distinguishes three kinds of meaning in Scripture: the literal, the allegorical, and the anagogical. These roughly correspond to the past, present and future meanings. Of course, Augustine says, Scripture has a literal meaning, a provenance, and a set of events to which it actually refers. This is its past meaning. There is then the way that Scripture inspires us in prayer,

and in faith, to a greater and richer understanding of the truth about God. God is so
incomprehensible that some of the truth
about him can only be understood poetically, or
through allusion. This is not the literal meaning, but the allegorical meaning of Scripture.
Here there is a speculative element – that we
should think beyond the literal meaning of a
given text or passage to what else it might
point towards, and to how it connects with
other parts of Scripture and to the Tradition
itself. This is a practice of interpretation which
has taken shape over centuries in the life of the
Church. It is the present meaning, the meaning of Scripture in the daily prayer of the
Church.

Finally there is the meaning of the text
which is directed to our salvation – this is the
future meaning, the 'anagogical' aspect.
'Anagogical' literally means whatever leads or
lifts us up: as far as Scripture is concerned this
is the way in which any given passage of
Scripture connects with the meaning of the
whole account given in Scripture of God's
offer of salvation to man through the saving

events around his Son. The future meaning of
Scripture is the meaning of Scripture not just
in the Church but *for* the Church, it is what
authenticates the Church's interpretation. The
authentic interpretation of Scripture in the
Church does not come from *within* Scripture alone, but from the *end* to which the
Church is destined, which is what She knows
through the Apostolic tradition – exactly
as Benedict himself has argued, against the
view that no doctrine of the Church can be
taught which is not immediately present in
Scripture.

One of the theologians to speak of this
richer and more authentic understanding of
Scripture was Henri de Lubac, who has written on the place of Scripture in the Mediaeval
Church, in contrast to modern methods of
exegesis. De Lubac only codifies and shows the
history of what any theologian who knows the
work of Aquinas or Bonaventure should
understand very well – that on the one hand
all the doctrines of the Church are implicit in
Scripture, but on the other, they are made
explicit by the Church's own practice and his-

tory of interpretation of Scripture, above all in its life of prayer – which means through the way it has used Scripture in the texts and prayers of the Mass and the other public prayer – the prayer of the Breviary – the prayer of the Church. It is these that school the ordinary believer in how the Church reads Scripture and understands it.

Benedict's underlying and fundamental concern is for the ordinary believer to continue to have access to Scripture. He has argued that the saints 'were often uneducated and, at any rate, knew nothing about exegetical contexts. Yet they were the ones who understood it best'. The same concern that manifests itself with regard to the dangers in the Sacred Liturgy and in the work of the Council can also be seen here – that the Scriptures became the province of experts, and so the ordinary faithful are left unable to trust what the Church has always taught concerning Scripture. Benedict argues that as far as the pure historical, scientific matters of biblical interpretation are concerned, here the experts and specialists are required. But the decisive meaning of the Bible is to be grasped by the one who has simple faith.

14

Divine Revelation

If it is to the simple person of faith that the Scriptures are really to speak, what does Benedict mean, and how will this happen? At its very heart, this question can be traced right back to Benedict's *Habilitation* studies on St. Bonaventure. Here the inner unity of the Scriptures and the Sacred Liturgy can be made manifest in their whole meaning – in Benedict's understanding of Divine Revelation, an understanding that was common to Mediaeval theology.

The idea that God's revelation of himself to man through his Son in the power of his Spirit is synonymous with the mere words of Scripture is, for Benedict totally insufficient. At the same time the idea that all that matters in the Sacred Liturgy is that Christ becomes present in the Mass when the 'words of consecration' are pronounced over bread and wine – and that all else is just beautiful ceremonies, added on to an objective event – is just as inadequate. The idea that the community can come together and express its common fellowship as an act of its own making, and can 'decide' what Scripture says, or that Christ has been truly present among them, is equally false as a description of God's self-disclosure in our worship. Again, the question of truth is paramount.

In his study of St. Bonaventure, Benedict had come to notice something about the Mediaeval understanding of God which, one might say, has even yet properly to be recovered. It is the central issue on which the Council had tried to touch, and which, I might suggest, is yet fully to have its moment of understanding. So much of contemporary theology has rested – and still does rest – on *doing*. Benedict himself has spoken of the ceaseless, restless activism of contemporary Christianity. Of course when we are so busied, and so surrounded by a noise of our own making, we are apt to overlook something, a thing which the Mediaevals knew all too well

and which Benedict had made much of in his
Habilitation thesis. Divine Revelation is God's
approach *toward* man. God's divine self-
disclosure – his revealing of himself, his *dis-
closing* of himself so that he can be seen to be
true, is *God's*, not *our*, initiative. Such an initiative does not lie around undiscovered for
when we can be still enough to notice it, it is
always *for*, and so *given to* some*one*.

In describing his thesis, Benedict notes that
'in Bonaventure (as well as in the theologians
of the thirteenth century) there was nothing
corresponding to our conception of "revelation", by which we are normally in the habit of
referring to all the revealed contents of the
faith'. Too often revelation has been taken as
simply the same thing as Scripture, or as 'con-
tained' in Tradition, as if it were immediately
obvious what that means. Revelation is an act
– an act of God's self-communication to man.
Earlier I noted that Holy Saturday, the day
between Good Friday and Easter Day, defines
the mode of faith and prayer. It is the historical and existential basis of anxious but joyful
anticipation of Christ. The Christian who lives

in faith and hope – therefore in this mood of joyful anticipation – is the one who will be ready for God's initiative of approach to him or her. Above all, however, the believer is part of the body of Christ. The real subject of revelation is the Church herself, in the person of her faithful, each of whom is a member of the body of Christ. The Church *lives* in the conversation between God the Father and the Son.

Coupled with this idea is that revelation is not what Scripture is, but what Scripture *contains*. Benedict says 'if Bonaventure is right, then revelation precedes Scripture and becomes deposited in Scripture but is not simply identical with it. This in turn means that revelation is always something greater than what is merely written down … Because an essential element of Scripture is the Church as understanding subject, and with this the fundamental sense of tradition already given'.

What is the context for God to reveal himself – where does God take the initiative which can be received by the one readied to attend to the God who speaks? Here we should offer a certain background. For in the period after the Enlightenment, in German romanticism especially, increasingly the idea had grown up that God could reveal himself anywhere and through anything. Emmanuel Kant (1724–1804) especially had suggested that the great 'sublime' moments in nature and art were revelations of the divine realm, and so God, even though as revelations they never came to mind as objects of consciousness, but were more like intuitions or feelings. Something like this is reflected in some of the paintings of Caspar David Friedrich (1774–1840) or the poetry of William Wordsworth (1770–1850). Karl Rahner's theology of 'anonymous Christians', those whose impulse towards righteousness and whose love of the truth seemed itself to be a gift of God and an indication of God having been manifest to and by them in some way also seems to point toward this idea.

For Benedict, however, it is clearly the work of the Sacred Liturgy in which God reveals himself in the person of his Son through his Holy Spirit to the believer who anticipates God's self-disclosure in faith and hope. The

Church's liturgy, as I noted earlier, is suffused with Scripture, so much so that I said that in many ways the Sacred Liturgy *is* the interpretation of Scripture belonging to the Church. Benedict understands this connection between the Sacred Liturgy and Scripture in the following way: 'Just as I learned to understand the New Testament as being the soul of all theology, so too I came to see the liturgy as being its living element, without which it would necessarily shrivel up.'

Here is why liturgy can never be 'made' – it is part of what is 'given' by God. It is here that the Pope has been concerned for the different understandings of the meaning of the liturgy that prevail in the Church in the present day: 'behind the various ways of understanding liturgy there are, as almost always, different ways of understanding the Church, and consequently God, and man's relation to him'. Benedict says of his own emerging understanding of the liturgy when young, 'here I was encountering a reality that no one had simply thought up, a reality that no official authority or great individual had created'. Anyone who has prayed the liturgy in its entirety – the hours of the Church intertwined with the Mass – will know how the interplay of its scriptural texts, their emphasis and suppression in diff-erent ways at different times of the day, the week, and the liturgical year, lead to an instinctual familiarity with the meaning of the texts (the Church's Tradition) that could not be got from simply reading the Bible as a book from end to end.

Here, therefore, is why Benedict has devoted so much energy to discussion and concern with the Sacred Liturgy, and why he has emphasized repeatedly the continuity between the liturgy as it was before the Second Vatican Council and the liturgy after 1970. Benedict has said only recently that 'it seems to me indispensable to continue to offer the oppor-tunity to continue to celebrate according to the old Missal [of before the Council] … what was fundamental before 1969 remains funda-mental afterwards … the Liturgy is the same'.

Does the Pope mean by this that Christ is unknown beyond the Church? It is not that God *could* not speak outside the Church, but rather that the Church is the recognized and guaranteed place wherein God always and continually makes himself present and discloses himself. If this ordinary and continual revealing of his truth were not happening, God's self-disclosure beyond the Church could not even be recognized for what it is – even when the Spirit blows beyond the bounds of the Church, that breath returns to the Church herself. The Church is the proper place of God's self-revelation to man, it is the *home* of this truth.

If we understand the Church as the place of God's self-disclosure to man, we can see that the Church is only an institution in a dependent sense – its institutional work is to safeguard and preserve God's continuing self-revelation. Here is why the Sacred Liturgy is of paramount importance, and why Benedict is likely to continue to pay close attention to it: and why he has said that Liturgy is not about us, but about God. Because God acts in this way, there is nothing man can do – except co-operate with the truth that is given.

15

Europe – 'One of the Great Subjects of Concern'

Timothy Garton Ash, one of Oxford University's leading experts in European history and affairs, said in April 2005 that 'atheists should welcome the election of Pope Benedict XVI, for this aged, scholarly, conservative, uncharismatic Bavarian will surely hasten precisely the de-Christianization of Europe that he aims to reverse. At the end of this papacy, Europe may again be as un-christian as it was when St. Benedict, one of the patron saints of Europe, founded his pioneering monastic order'.

Garton Ash is not alone in this verdict: many of the Indian, Asian or African students I have taught or given lectures to in Belgium or Britain – often priests or members of Catholic religious orders – have taken a view not far from this. The future of Catholicism, and of Christianity more widely, is not in Europe, they have argued. When Benedict was elected I was in the United States, a guest of a seminary where many held high hopes of welcoming the first Latin American pope, or perhaps the first African pope for several hundred years. A glum face at breakfast the next day asked me 'why did it have to be a European, since the Church in Europe is finished?'

Is the Church in Europe to be written off, and is faith in Europe destined to be no more than a private affair, good enough at the personal level so that being part of the Church is little more than being a member of a private club or a history society? Is there no more to be done for it in this cradle of Christianity's expansion? This is a question that is central both to the decision of the conclave and to Benedict's thought itself. It is perhaps the most important question the Pope has addressed and will continue to have to address. It was not less important for his predecessor.

The events of John Paul II's death, up to his funeral, were extraordinary – millions, especially of the young, flocked to Rome to be part of the mourning and to witness in whatever way they could, the burial of the dead Pope – billions watched both the funeral, the events of the conclave, and Benedict's inaugural Mass. In the days and weeks after John Paul II's death, the churches in Europe were full: not less full were the pages of the European press. A newspaper cartoon in Britain asked 'since when was Britain a Catholic country?' Christianity is by no means 'over' in Europe. In exactly the same way that there is something to be decided for the whole world in the unrolling of the phenomenon of global economic expansion (so-called globalization), so there is something to be decided for the whole spiritual future of the world in what unfolds in Europe.

Metz said of Garton Ash's provocative remarks 'unfortunately he couldn't free himself from the negative Ratzinger-clichés of the British high-street'. What Metz points to is the way in which the spokesmen of secular society consistently misunderstand and misinterpret both the place of religion in Western life, and in particular, they misunderstand the effect of Benedict's election – the instinctive understanding of it – that many Catholics, and many ordinary men and women, even those to some extent sceptical of the man, will have. Does Benedict have a blueprint for the recovery of an understanding of Christendom in European life? He has certainly spoken of the idea of Christendom, notably in questioning the accession of Turkey to the European Union, as a country which, traditionally Islamic, is not genuinely European. In his inaugural homily Benedict said 'there is no need for me to present a programme of governance'. He was primarily referring to the Church, but much more aptly could this be said of the Church's attitude to the West. It is not the Church's role to govern – that belongs to politicians. It *is* the Church's task to call the governors to account for their actions under God, and to illuminate the spiritual and Christian consequences of their thinking.

Nicholas Boyle, a Catholic and an academic commenting in Britain shortly after Benedict's election, has argued that in the Church in general, and for Benedict in particular, 'above all there is the absence of a foundation for any instinctive understanding of the commercial, industrial, and financial world, the circle of investment, employment, production, and consumption, which determines the billions of lives to which the Vatican Council sought to address its message of joy and hope'. He questions the capability of Benedict to comment on the political future of Europe and the world, and yet, in doing so, he draws attention to the way in which even very faithful and intelligent Catholics – let alone everyone else – have taken for granted that it is economic might and not the love and redemptive mercy of God that is the driving force in social life. To paraphrase Benedict's critique of Liberation Theology – if we accept Boyle's argument then we accept the Marxist message (that the world is determined by its economic fortunes) without even espousing the Marxist hope – that the world can be better through economic management. All the Church can do here is console the poor and admonish the rich in the drive for economic progress.

It is here that Benedict returns us to the situation of Benedict XV's election of 1914, of a

world coming to terms with unbridled economic progress, in which spiritual depth is
consistently erased for the sake of pure economic value. Spiritual depth? The Germans
call it *Geist*, which means the fundamental
meaning of life itself, and it is not insignificant
that so erased is this idea already that we
English-speakers barely have a word that says
what *Geist* indicates. If Benedict has no blueprint, no plan of governance, what does he
offer, in the decisive spiritual battle-ground of
Europe, and to the wider world, and that goes
beyond mere consolation of the poor and
admonition of the rich?

In May 2004 Benedict was invited to
address members of the Italian Senate by its
Head, the philosopher Marcello Pera (1943–).
Benedict's speech, given in the Library of the
Senate, has a most remarkable feature. He
described the history of Europe as the interaction of forms of government and the Church.
In the speech Benedict traces a whole history
of Europe, from its origins in ancient Greece
seeking to distinguish itself from oriental
Persia, through the various forms of the

Roman Empire, the Norse kingdoms, the sep-
arate development of Byzantium, flowering of
scholarship in Mediaeval Christendom, the
Turkish invasions, the Renaissance and
Enlightenment, the French Revolution, the
development of the North and South Americas,
industrialization, the secularizations of the
liberal-bourgeois revolutions of the nineteenth century, through the totalitarianisms of
the twentieth and up to the present day. This is
an account more usually (especially since the
Second World War – indeed, as it is taught in
our schools) of economic, social, and scientific
progress. Told like this, history is understood
as Marx understood it, without his apocalyp-
tic revolutionary vision. Indeed, it can be told
like that (and it should, it is not wrongly
expressed like this) – but Europe has been
something else as well.

John Paul II gave his account of the development of Europe in the Encyclical *Fides et
Ratio* as a history of the development of ideas
– in this he borrowed heavily from the kind of
understanding of intellectual and philosophical development that began with Hegel

(1770–1831) and was unfolded spectacularly by Martin Heidegger. Described in this way, as Pope John Paul II says – eventually in Europe, and after so much progress, 'something like nihilism arises' and has to be addressed. The euphoria of nihilism is precisely what most people understand instinctively about their own lives and the lives around them. It is an account that explains to us at the deepest level the fact that, dare we once think about the meaning of the world we are in, we find ourselves on a precipice, with nothing beneath us. Again, the account *should* be given like this – it is where, and this means *who*, we are today. It is what Garton Ash is trying to name, correctly, and what he wrongly tries to celebrate. Benedict has said of this understanding that the collapse of meaning in the social context inevitably leads to totalitarianism. He has seen this at first hand.

This is why Benedict accounted for the history of Europe as the interaction of forms of government and the Church. He describes it, in other words, as an understanding of the intimate interlinking of social structures and the structure of faith and revelation – the form that social life takes and the way that we are governed, with the form of redemption as it manifests itself in history – which is the Church. For the Pope to understand the history of Europe, of America, and of the West's decisive influence on the world like this is an astonishing and rich engagement with history which is at the same time its most authentic account. This is Europe's, the West's, and the whole of mankind's, most authentic future – the future in the God made manifest in Jesus Christ, through the activity of the Spirit. It is at the same time the story the Church must learn – and re-learn – how to tell. It is the engagement of the Church with the world that is the (as yet only just begun) authentic interpretation of the Second Vatican Council. This is the task that has lurked in Benedict's intellectual development, in his theological writing, and now, we should hope, which will become manifest in his papacy.

If the Church has no plan of governance for the world, how will this understanding be disclosed? In May 2004 Benedict had a most remarkable encounter at the Bavarian Catholic Academy with the philosopher Jürgen Habermas (1929–). Habermas, academically a Marxist, has been one of the most influential figures in the intellectual self-understanding of Europe, the West, and Germany, in the post-war period. A thinker and philosopher of the Frankfurt School, his early work is full of the optimism and energy of the post-war reconstruction of the European West. If there were a 'pope' of atheistic modernity, he would be foremost among its *papabile*. Increasingly, Habermas has spoken of the post-secular status of Europe, by which he means the collapse of that intellectual optimism in favour of a banal drive for sheer economic development devoid of wider meaning.

Habermas has argued that 'Christianity, and nothing else, is the ultimate foundation of liberty, conscience, human rights, and democracy, the benchmarks of Western civilization'. Habermas is unlikely to seek membership of the Catholic Church, but he has increasingly wanted to enter into a deep confrontation with what he sees as the primary source of meaning in the West. What is almost more important than what was exchanged between Benedict and Habermas is the fact of the exchange – of a kind almost unthinkable twenty years before. It shows a readiness for openness to a wider understanding of truth – a readiness precipitated by exactly the situation outlined by John Paul II – but which cannot work out responses to this situation alone. Is this not the exact present situation of the West? Is this not the place to which we have come, and for which we have been given this Pope?

16

In the Social Sphere –
Truth – What is That?

Just a few weeks before the death of John Paul II, Benedict published a small book in the Herder *Spektrum* series entitled *Values in Times of Radical Change*, whose main theme is the place of, and decisions over, Europe. In many ways the little book is an expansion of the speech he gave in the library of the Italian Senate. In this book Benedict can be seen in profound confrontation (as he was with Jürgen Habermas) with other apostles of postmodernity – among them the American philosopher Richard Rorty (1931–).

The spectre with which Benedict has confronted Europe and the West is its slow but sure dissolution. Benedict has said, in a speech at the end of 2004, 'A society in which God is completely absent self-destructs. We saw this in the great totalitarian regimes of the last century'. He has drawn particular attention to the collapsing birth-rate in Europe, to the place of the family. He was quick after his election to reiterate his commitment to the Church's teaching on abortion and euthanasia, precisely because they are signs of the Church's unflinching proclamation of the dignity of human life. He is likely to continue to have an acute and sensitive understanding of sexual ethics – he noted wryly in a recent speech that at the very point where marriage as an institution is collapsing, it is being sought for couples of the same sex. He understands the importance of marriage and the family to be not only a physical, but a moral guarantee of the future of society.

More important even than these questions is that of the meaning of political life. Benedict has said 'in political life, it seems almost indecent to speak of God, as if it were an attack on the freedom of those who do not believe. The world of politics follows its norms and paths, excluding God as something that does not belong to this world. The same in the world of business, the economy, and private life. God remains marginalized'.

How does he understand the connection in political life, between the absence of God and the renewed spectre of collapse and even totalitarianism? The connection has much to do with the direction of economic life. Benedict has noted the prosperity of the West is uneven, and has been bought at the cost of the poverty of the majority of the world's population. Yet the West will be decisive, precisely *because* the developments in social society have followed from an unbridled prosperity that is already arriving in its effects (even if not in fact) in every country in the world. In other words, the spectre before us is a tyranny that arises out of our very prosperity – we are simply too comfortable to ask wider and deeper questions, questions which have consequences for the health and welfare of others. Others in poorer nations, drawn more poorly in to the life we have in abundance, will suffer because of our prosperous lack of any concern for deeper ends.

Benedict has already rejected, and forcefully so, the response of the politicization of Christianity, as it was for a few years held out by the Liberation Theologians. The question, he suggests, is one of truth. The tyranny of wealth is either the tyranny of a wealthy majority, or a tyranny of those who become the majority through the concentration of the power in their hands. How will this tyranny manifest itself, and how can it be shown to relate to truth?

In *Values in Times of Radical Change*, Benedict meditates on the trial of Jesus before Pilate – the point at which Pilate washes his hands of responsibility, the point at which he asks 'Truth? What is that?' Benedict points out that Pilate – who is not a bad man – is nevertheless crushed by the cries of the majority. He draws attention to an exegesis of this text undertaken by the protestant theologian Heinrich Schlier (1900–1978) at the moment of the Nazi accession to power. In Pilate's question, at that very moment, truth becomes for him something unreachable. Pilate is confronted not by truth, but by the need to conform to a pure expression of political power. Benedict notes with some irony that in his decision to crucify Jesus to satisfy the cries of the crowd, 'Pilate has acted as a fully developed democrat'.

Benedict's point is not that democracy is disastrous, nor is he 'anti-democratic'. He simply notes that democracy and truth are not identical. At the point where Pilate cannot reach the truth, he fails to understand that truth is not rule of the majority. For the answer to Pilate is made by Jesus himself: the Lord reminds Pilate that his power is not from the state, nor from the crowd, but 'from above'. Schlier's point is that every attempt to set faith and the people or the state on the same basis will fail: all power is ultimately of God, or it is nothing, and it cannot be true. The unity of truth and power is known only in God. And, we may add, the unity of truth and power in God is most visible in the Crucified One, the one who offers himself for the sake of the World.

Christianity's task is to inform political power by restoring its relation to truth. This can never be by the simple means of saying that truth is guaranteed by the democratic process. Truth in the political sphere is deliberative – it is decided through the relation and interplay of interests, of political argument, of the parties concerned. Democracy is a way of doing this, but when reduced to a tyranny of the majority it becomes no more just or true than any other form of government, of which tyranny and totalitarian oppression are the worst forms.

To erase God from political deliberation is therefore to close democracy's access to truth. Benedict argues that not even the desire for the state and for politics to be rational will be enough to maintain the essential relation to truth. He quotes Aldous Huxley (1894–1963), as one who understood the standard of rationality, of what is reasonable for action and for the political process, to be founded on the basis of scientific and technical progress – man should be (for Huxley and for modern society), in his innermost, a rational product. Benedict replies that 'only if we see here an Absolute, that stands over all deliberations concerning the good, do we really act ethically and not calculatingly'.

What then, is the task of the Christian in Europe, and beyond it? The Christian is not merely to contribute to the economic, progressive well-being of the world. Because he is one who has been addressed by God – one who is brought to life *in* God (through his being shaped by God's continued self-disclosure, above all in the activity of the Church, in its liturgy and prayer) – because the Christian knows God in Christ *personally*, the Christian in his public life *is* the real doer of truth, the 'truth capacity', Benedict calls him, of the world. The Christian is the one who understands what is good and right, and can explain it. The Christian – because God is the life of the world and reveals himself to be this through Christ his Son, the eternal world – is the world's capability of knowing life and truth itself, life in its fullness, eternal life in its truth.

FOUR

Conclusion – and the Real beginning

17

Ending at the Beginning

As Benedict's papacy begins, what will he look forward to, and what are his priorities likely to be? Benedict is, as much as his predecessor, a man of the Church. But, as we have seen in his understanding of how the Church is and how it unfolds in history, he does not see the Church primarily as an institution. Benedict has been critical of those whose theological outlook has been dominated by 'ecclesiocentrism', placing the Church as an institution too much in the centre of its own concerns. He has taken to task some of the ways in which the Church can appear to look in on itself – even in the way that priest and people now often face each other at Mass, instead of priest and people alike 'facing God'. The Church, for him, looks out: out towards God, first; out next for the sake of the redemption of the world.

Above all, the Church is where God discloses himself in his Truth, and that means his Son, to the world, where that disclosure is completed and fulfilled.

As such, the Church has faith – the anxious mood of joyful anticipation that characterizes Holy Saturday, the day grounded in the anguish and the drama of Good Friday and the Sacrifice of Christ: the day that looks forward to meeting with the Lord who has already risen, the anticipation that is the condition for, and character of, prayer. Benedict has said that this anticipation is what it means to be prophetic – this is how prophecy is borne out of prayer. And the Church prays – which does not mean, sends up endless petitions to God in busyness, but means, waits on the Word of God, and waits to be given the words with which to address all nations, all men of goodwill: this is her prophetic work.

It is likely that Benedict will, in various ways, turn his attention to the Sacred Liturgy during his pontificate. Many noted a renewed solemnity in both the funeral Mass for John Paul II, over which Benedict presided as Dean

of the College of Cardinals, and his own inaugural Mass. He has written and said so much
on the place of the liturgy – reinforcing the
assertion of the Second Vatican Council that
the liturgy is the summit of the activity of the
Church, and the fount from which Christ's
power in the Church flows. There are signs that
he will renew the efforts to end the schisms over
the reform of the liturgy, perhaps by making
much greater accommodation for those (myself
included) attached to the pre-1970 rites of the
Church. By restoring the understanding of the
continuity in the Church's practices before
and after the Second Vatican Council, is this
how he will ensure there is an authentic return
to the texts of that Council, and so usher in a
new and more mature period of reflection and
reception of the Council itself?

Is there not an indication here of the way in
which the Council's history will unfold? That
the Church, having re-engaged with the world
and having discovered – at huge cost to itself –
how much a part of the world she has become,
to the point, at times of so dissolving herself into
the world that she has all but lost the ability to

distinguish between herself and the world, must now lead that world into which she has been dissolved back to God? Is this not what it means to be the salt of the earth, the leaven in the lump, historically speaking? Is this not how the history of the Council will cease to be one of decline and collapse, and become one of growth and rebirth?

The Mass with which Benedict's papacy proper began – the inaugural Mass – indicated several marks of the papacy to come: beginning as it did in the *Confessio*, the place of the tomb of St. Peter, that Benedict is Successor of Peter, Prince of the Apostles. Benedict has said that 'I set out from where Peter was laid down'. The Pallium – the yoke of lamb's and sheep's wool which Benedict assumed in a new form in the inaugural Mass – represents 'the lost, sick or weak sheep which the shepherd lays on his shoulders', but also the parable of the lost sheep, which is 'an image of the mystery of Christ and the Church'. The ring of the fisherman which Benedict put on in this Mass reminds us that 'we are living in alienation, in the salt waters of suffering and death; in a sea

174

of darkness without light. The net of the Gospel pulls us out of the waters of death and brings us into the splendour of God's light, into true life. It is really true'.

In his homily Benedict commented that the task of the Church is to be alive, because God does not and cannot 'abandon humanity in so wretched a condition'. The Church, therefore, is *of* God and *for* the world.

Regarding the tasks that lie before him, Benedict stressed especially ecumenism, the need to enter friendship and communion with other Churches in the East, and Christians in the West, those who have received baptism 'but are not yet in full communion'. Benedict has made several references to the need to be in open dialogue with non-Catholic Christians. More than these, the Pope especially mentioned the ongoing dialogue with 'my brothers and sisters of the Jewish people, to whom we are joined by a great shared spiritual heritage, one rooted in God's irrevocable promises'. Thirdly he has spoken of how 'like a wave gathering force, my thoughts go out to all men and women of today, to believers and non-believers alike'.

Benedict has given a special emphasis to the young – so many of whom were drawn into the Church at the call of Pope John Paul II, and who turned up in their millions in Rome after his death. It is likely that this emphasis will continue. The annual event of 'World Youth Day' will continue to have the significance for the papacy it attained under John Paul II.

Above all this will be a papacy of dialogue. Dialogue does not here mean talk, or the suppression of talk for fear of offence. Benedict is one, more than most, who is unafraid of disputing issues of the most serious kind, issues that touch the heart, both of people and of society as a whole. He is unafraid of the consequences of disagreement and dispute. It is often through an open encounter with our differences that the truth can become seen for what it is. The dialogue he is likely to seek, gently, as is his personal manner, will be a discussion of matters of life, and death, and what succeeds death: of truth itself, and He who is the Truth. Dialogue over Europe, dialogue with a world that this Pope believes, above all, should find its home in God, or as Benedict

himself encourages us: 'Yes, open, open wide
the doors to Christ – and you will find true
life.'

18

Bibliography of Benedict's Published Works in English Translation

A New Song for the Lord: Faith in Christ and Liturgy Today, Herder and Herder, New York, 1997.

A Turning Point for Europe? The Church in the Modern World, Ignatius Press, San Francisco, 1994.

Behold the Pierced One: An Approach to a Spiritual Christology, Ignatius Press, San Francisco, 1987.

Being Christian, Franciscan Herald Press, Chicago, 1970.

Called to Communion: Understanding the Church Today, Ignatius Press, San Francisco, 1996.

Church Ecumenism and Politics: New Essays in Ecclesiology, St. Paul's Press, Slough, 1988.

Co-Workers of the Truth: Meditations for Every Day of the Year, Ignatius Press, San Francisco, 1992.

Crisis in the Church, Catholic Truth Society, London, 1980.

Daughter of Zion: Meditations on the Church's Marian Belief, Ignatius Press, San Francisco, 1983.

Dogma and Preaching, Franciscan Herald Press, Chicago, 1983.

Eschatology: Death and Eternal Life, Catholic University of America, Washington DC, 1988.

Faith and the Future, Franciscan Herald Press, Chicago, 1971.

God and the World: Believing and Living in Our Time: A Conversation with Peter Seewald, Ignatius Press, San Francisco, 2002.

God is Near Us: The Eucharist the Heart of Life, Ignatius Press, San Francisco, 2003.

God of Jesus Christ, Franciscan Herald Press, Chicago, 1978.

Gospel, Catechesis, Catechism: Sidelights on the Catechism of the Catholic Church, Ignatius Press, San Francisco, 1997.

In the Beginning: A Catholic Understanding of the Story of Creation and the Fall (Resourcement), W. B. Eerdmans Publishing Co., Indiana, 1995 (1990).

Introduction to Christianity, Ignatius Press, San Francisco, 2004 (1969).

Introduction to the Catechism of the Catholic Church (with Christoph Cardinal Schönborn OP), Ignatius Press, San Francisco, 1994.

Journey Towards Easter: Retreat Given in the Vatican in the Presence of Pope John Paul II, St. Paul's Press, Slough, 1987.

Living with the Church, Franciscan Herald Press, Chicago, 1978.

Many Religions – One Covenant: Israel, the

Church and the World, Ignatius Press, San Francisco, 1999.

Milestones: Memoirs, Ignatius Press, San Francisco, 1998.

Ministers of Your Joy: Meditations on Priestly Spirituality, St. Paul's, Slough, 1989.

Pilgrim Fellowship of Faith: The Church as Communion, Ignatius Press, San Francisco, 2005.

Principles of Catholic Theology: Building Stones for a Fundamental Theology, Ignatius Press, San Francisco, 1987.

Principles of Christian Morality (with Hans Urs Cardinal von Balthasar), Ignatius Press, San Francisco, 1986.

Revelation and Tradition, Burns and Oates, London, 1965.

Salt of the Earth: The Church at the End of the Millennium: An Interview with Peter Seewald, Ignatius Press, San Francisco, 1997.

Seek that which is Above: Meditations Through the Year, Ignatius Press, San Francisco, 1986.

Seeking God's Face, Franciscan Herald Press, Chicago, 1982.

The Catholic Priest as Moral Teacher and Guide, Ignatius Press, San Francisco, 1966.

The Episcopate and the Primacy (with Karl Rahner SJ), Burns and Oates, Edinburgh, 1962.

The Feast of Faith: Approaches to a Theology of the Liturgy, Ignatius Press, San Francisco, 1986.

The God of Jesus Christ: Meditations on God in the Trinity, Franciscan Herald Press, Chicago, 1978.

The Meaning of Christian Brotherhood, Ignatius Press, San Francisco, 1993 (1966).

The Nature and Mission of Theology: Essays to Orient Theology in Today's Debates, Ignatius Press, San Francisco, 1995.

The Ratzinger Report: An Interview on the State of the Church, Ignatius Press, San Francisco, 1985.

The Sabbath of History, Jaca Books, Washington, 2001.

The Spirit of the Liturgy, Ignatius Press, San Francisco, 2000.

Theology of History in St. Bonaventure, Franciscan Herald Press, Chicago, 1989 (1971).

To Look on Christ: Exercises in Faith Hope and Love, St. Paul's, Slough, 1991.

Two Say Why. Why I am Still a Christian. Why I am Still in the Church (with Hans Urs Cardinal von Balthasar), Franciscan Herald Press, Chicago, 1971.

Truth and Tolerance: Christian Belief and World Religions, Ignatius Press, San Francisco, 2004.